GRANDMA MOSES

The Artist
Behind
the Myth

1. Grandma Moses in her flower garden. 1953. Photograph by Otto Kallir.

GRANDMA MOSES

THE ARTIST BEHIND THE MYTH

JANE KALLIR

CLARKSON N. POTTER, INC. / PUBLISHERS, NEW YORK

DISTRIBUTED BY CROWN PUBLISHERS, INC.

IN ASSOCIATION WITH

GALERIE ST. ETIENNE, NEW YORK

Front cover: *A Beautiful World*. 1948.

Back cover: *A Beautiful World* (detail).

All paintings by Grandma Moses reproduced herein are executed in oil on Masonite or cardboard, unless otherwise specified. Where appropriate, captions also include the numerical listing in Otto Kallir's catalogue raisonné, *Grandma Moses* (Harry N. Abrams, Inc., 1973).

Inquiries should be addressed to Clarkson N. Potter, Inc., Publishers, One Park Avenue, New York, New York 10016
Published simultaneously in Canada by General Publishing Company Limited

Library of Congress Cataloging in Publication Data

Kallir, Jane.
  Grandma Moses : the artist behind the myth.
  Issued in conjunction with an exhibition held at the Galerie St. Etienne, New York, Nov. 16, 1982-Jan. 8, 1983.
  Includes bibliographical references and index.
  1. Moses, Grandma, 1860-1961. 2. Painters—United States—Biography. I. Moses, Grandma, 1860-1961. II. Galerie St. Etienne. III. Title.
ND237.M78K27 1982   759.13 [B]   82-7683
AACR2
ISBN 0-517-54748-1 (Clarkson N. Potter edition—hardcover)
ISBN 0-910810-21-4 (Galerie St. Etienne edition—paper)

To those who never understood, and to my grandfather, who always did

Photographs by Geoffrey Clements: Front Cover; Plates 83, 88, 106, 135, 169.

Photographs by Eric Pollitzer: Plates 73, 78, 98, 108, 114, 120, 141, 148, 156, 160, 165, 174, 179.

Detail photography by Jane Kallir

Designed by Gary Cosimini

Printed by Rapoport Printing Corp., New York

CONTENTS

2. **Haying Time.** 1945. 24″ x 30″. (K. 485).

INTRODUCTION

In October 1940 my grandfather, Otto Kallir, gave a one-woman exhibition to an unknown farmwife from upstate New York. Having left Europe less than a year earlier, he was himself new to New York art circles. His Manhattan gallery was chiefly a showplace for the art of his native Austria, but the paintings of this woman intrigued him, for they evidenced a freshness that was lacking in much American art of the time. As sometimes happens, he saw with the eyes of a foreigner what many Americans, blinded by their proximity, had failed to see.

The artist's rise to prominence was not, as was later said, meteoric. Something about her work and her personality captured the American imagination; it took hold, and it slowly grew. By the end of the decade she was hailed as the nation's grandmother, had met the president, been featured in *Time, Life, Look* and *The New York Times* magazines innumerable times, and was the subject of a book and a film. Her homespun paintings were shown from coast to coast and reproduced on millions of Christmas cards. Throughout the 1950s, her fame grew unabated, while critics argued over the merits of her work and the reasons for her extraordinary success.

Grandma Moses was one of those rare artists whose appeal cut across the class distinctions that usually separate "high" from "popular" art. In an era dominated by celebrities of every stripe, she was among the few painters who evoked a broad, general response from the American public. Beloved by almost everyone, she was increasingly scorned by that segment of the cultural elite that equated popularity with inferiority. Ironically, in an age of "anything-goes art," the little old lady from Eagle Bridge, New York, became controversial.

It has now been over twenty years since the artist's death in 1961 at the age of 101. In these years, her achievement has

3. **Haying Time** (detail).

often been questioned, the questions seldom answered. How did she get to be so remarkably famous? Was it simply the human-interest appeal of her heartwarming story? Was it her extreme old age? Her folksy personality? Was she the pawn of slick publicity people? And, last but most important, was she a good artist?

This book attempts to answer these questions from the perspective provided by the passage of time. A phenomenon like Grandma Moses sheds light on our entire cultural system, prompting us to challenge the sources of both fame and greatness, and the qualities that distinguish

4. Wood engraving with Moses' pencil outlining, taken from a children's book. Approximately 4⅛" x 5½". Moses' stylized figures (Plate 5) were influenced by popular illustrations such as this.

5. **Haying Time** (detail, Plate 2).

the two. It is significant that the years of Moses' ascendancy—1940–1961—are the same as those in which American abstraction came to dominate the international art market. One of the purposes of this study is to probe the connections between these two developments, for the triumph of the avant-garde was a contributing factor in the relegation of Grandma Moses to the junk pile of popular culture. While the structure of our cultural hierarchy provides one point of reference for the Moses saga, another is poignantly reflected in the yearnings and dreams of the American people as a whole. To a public benumbed by a pervasive fear of atomic holocaust, Moses was akin to that bright, ethereal creature, Hope, fluttering out of Pandora's box after all its evil contents had been released. Now that those anxiety-ridden years have begun to fade into history, along with the era of the American avant-garde and the story of Grandma Moses, we can see more easily that Moses herself had a history as heir to a long tradition of American folk art. Her story, the story of folk art, and the story of abstract art are three cultural strands that became strangely entangled during the forties and fifties. The untangling of them herein, it is hoped, will provide the reader with a clearer way of looking at all the art involved.

Moses' artistic achievement must stand or fall on its own

6.
**Haying
Time**
(detail,
Plate 2).

merits, but a better understanding of it is facilitated by an analysis of its immediate cultural environment and its origins in the nineteenth-century folk tradition. The first part of this study thus focuses on a reexamination of the Moses legend: her life in fact and myth. The second segment relates her achievements to those of her folk predecessors and contemporaries. Finally, the concluding three chapters of the book present a pictorial essay juxtaposing detailed close-ups of her paintings with their iconographic sources to probe the artist's stylistic development.

In preparing this book, I have been privileged to have access to much previously unpublished material: letters by Grandma Moses, letters written to her by her various patrons, and a twelve-volume scrapbook documenting her critical reception by the press. Of crucial significance was the discovery, after many years of searching, of the sketches and source material (Plate 4) used by the artist to evolve her imagery. Though recently there has been increased research into the origins of folk styles, these efforts have often been hindered by a paucity of evidence. Thus an in-depth study of a folk painter similar to the examinations routinely accorded academic artists has never so far been possible. That the folk artist, no less than the academician, benefits from such an approach is made clear by the insights derived from Moses' preliminary drawings and clippings. I will always be deeply grateful to Will Moses, the artist's great-grandson, for preserving this material and making it available to me.

Needless to say, a project of this kind is never the effort of a single person, and I would therefore like to convey my thanks to the many who have helped me: to my grandmother, Fanny Kallir; to Hildegard Bachert, a Moses "veteran" of some forty years, who assisted my grandfather on his many books just as she has now assisted me on this one and who, among other things, wrote the chronology; to Martha Eaton, who generously put her father's unpublished manuscript on Grandma Moses at my disposal; and to the owners of the paintings reproduced herein. I would also like to express my gratitude to all the people connected with the production of the book: to Carolyn Hart, my editor, and especially to Teresa Nicholas, for diligence and kindness above and beyond the call of duty; to Gary Cosimini, who is far more than just the designer; and to our printer, Sidney Rapoport, an artist in his own right. Finally, mention must be made of the late Herbert Michelman, editor extraordinaire, who several years ago had the courage to publish my first book, without which there would never have been another.

7. **Applebutter Making.** 1947. 19¼″ x 23¼″. Galerie St. Etienne, New York. (K. 654). The painting depicts the "Dudley Place," one of the Virginia farms occupied by the Moses family in the 1890s.

CHAPTER ONE

THE MAKING OF A LEGEND

The First Eighty Years

Once upon a time, in the village of Eagle Bridge, just six miles west of the New York-Vermont border and twenty-five miles north of the town of Troy, there lived an elderly widow named Anna Mary Robertson Moses. When she was a very small child, before she even realized she had a proper name, her parents had called her Sissy. Eventually she grew into her full name, Anna Mary, which was shortened to Molly by her sister Winona, and Mary by her husband Thomas.[1] She and Thomas had ten children together, of whom five died in infancy. Those who lived to adulthood bore more children, who in turn bore more children. Anna Mary became a grandmother eleven times over, yet still she was known to many as Mother Moses. To the younger generations she was, very naturally, Grandma Moses.

In the child Sissy and the woman Anna Mary there had developed a love of beauty that would not find explicit expression until the mother became a grandmother and the need to pursue "useful" activities diminished. Born in 1860, at a time when education was a sometime thing ("three months in summer, three in winter"[2]), Anna Mary Robertson did not even dream of obtaining formal art training. The closest she ever came at the one-room district school she attended was the geography lesson. "The teacher would give us maps to draw, and I would make the mountains in my own way, the teacher liked them and would ask if he might keep them"[3] (Plate 8). At home, there were sometimes bits of slate, old windowpanes, and sheets of paper on which to draw or paint. "My oldest brother loved to draw steam engines,"

Anna Mary recalled. "The next brother went in for animals, but as for myself, I had to have pictures and the gayer the better."[4] The child's enthusiasm for "pictures" (as opposed to the single subjects that attracted her brothers) foreshadows the concern with total composition that would characterize her adult paintings. Anna Mary's father, who himself had artistic inclinations, encouraged the girl, "but Mother was more practical, thought I could spend my time in other ways."[5]

Thus Anna Mary's artistic aspirations were nipped in the bud. She came to share her mother's appreciation of fruitful labor, voluntarily leaving home at the age of twelve to earn her living as a "hired girl" on a neighboring farm. Such work, which involved every aspect of household management, was to occupy her for the next fifteen years, until the hired woman met a hired man, Thomas Salmon Moses, whom she married.

It had always been Thomas's dream to strike out on his own. Having heard that there were opportunities a-plenty in the post-Civil War South, he headed there with his bride. Anna Mary was taking no chances, though, and made sure she left her home in upstate New York with enough of her own savings to get back if anything went wrong.[6] As it turned out, the couple found a lovely farm near Staunton, Virginia, and Anna Mary invested her money in a cow. Many years later the now famous painter would say jokingly of that cow, "She was the foundation of my million dollars."[7] Anna Mary put the cow to good use, starting a butter-making operation that grew to accommodate a volume of 160 pounds a week.

"Always wanted to be independent," she wrote. "I couldn't bear the thought of sitting down and Thomas handing out the money."[8] It is evident that Anna Mary kept track of her own finances; when Thomas borrowed from her, she charged him interest.[9] From the start, she viewed their marriage as an equal partnership. "When we got married, I said, 'now we're a team, I must pull the load just the same as you do,' and so we commenced that way."[10] At one point she admitted that, within the hierarchy that governs any family, "I was the boss."[11]

After a number of years as tenants on different farms, the couple saved enough money to buy their own place. Thomas, however, always a little homesick for New York, was not eager to see his family grow deep roots in the fertile Virginia soil. In 1905, after selling the farm, they returned North, settling not far from Anna Mary's birthplace.

As her children grew up and left home to start their own families, Mother Moses was able to dabble in artistic projects for the first time since she herself was a child. Initially there was an element of chance in these ventures. Once, she ran out of wallpaper, so she decided to decorate a fireboard with a landscape (Plate 33). Another time, her husband brought her an old window from a caboose, suggesting that it could be painted on both sides. Always thrifty, Moses one day salvaged a bit of canvas from an old threshing-machine cover to paint on (Plate 45). The real impetus to make images came when her daughter Anna, who had seen an embroidered picture somewhere, asked for one like it. This "worsted" yarn piece was a great success, and Moses received requests for more. Though happy to comply, she became increasingly concerned about the impermanence of the medium, which was subject to the ravages of moths and faded after prolonged exposure to sunlight. Arthritis made it difficult for her to wield a needle, and when her sister Celestia commented that it might be less painful to paint, she readily took to the suggestion.

After her husband's death in 1927, Moses continued to make pictures for friends and family but did not consider turning to painting as a full-time occupation. She supplemented the family income by taking boarders into the sprawling farmhouse she shared with her son Hugh and his wife Dorothy, and with the help of her daughter-in-law, she raised chickens. Painting was something Grandma did "for pleasure, to keep busy and pass the time away, but I thought no more of it than of doing fancy work. When I had quite a few on hand, someone suggested that I take them down to the old Thomas' drug store in Hoosick Falls, so I tried that. I also exhibited a few at the Cambridge Fair with some canned fruits and raspberry jam. I won a prize for my fruit and jam, but no pictures."[12]

Mrs. Thomas, who owned the store, wanted to establish a sort of women's exchange, an outlet where local homemakers could sell their goods. Remembering Moses' pictures, which she had seen several years earlier at a charity sale, she invited her to participate.[13] Thus it was that, during Easter week in 1938, a civil engineer from New York City on vacation with his wife and daughter chanced upon the paintings of Grandma Moses in a drugstore window. This man, Louis J. Caldor, was an amateur art collector, and as his job gave him ample opportunity to travel, he always had an eye open for new discoveries. Caldor saw four paintings in the window, and when he asked the manager of the store if there were any more,

> he said he had the rest of the original consignment in the back storeroom for over a year. All in all, a dozen or so, and not a single sale in all that time. I told him I was most definitely interested, so he pulled all the pictures out of both the show-window and the storeroom, and spread them out on a shelf in the back of the store.... Although my two traveling companions were not much interested in Grandma's pictures, I liked them at once. Also, the prices were so low that I could not understand why not a single one had ever been sold.... The druggist said he was wishing he could interest me in the whole lot, since I liked...the pictures so much at first sight. Would I take them all if he knocked about ten percent off the total?[14]

The deal was struck, and Caldor left the drugstore with twelve to fourteen canvases and Grandma's address, in search of the artist. When finally he met her, she and her family "all listened to our conversation 'pop-eyed' with amazement, even disbelief, when I told Grandma not to worry anymore."[15]

Caldor, a man who approached everything with great intensity, zealously undertook to help Grandma Moses in every way he could. He had left Eagle Bridge that day with a promise to return soon and often, and within a month he had sent her a "regulation artist's sketching box" complete with a selection of canvas boards in various sizes. He continued to buy her paintings, to give her "pep talks," and to try to interest others in her work. Even after a year of fruitless effort on her behalf, his faith remained unshakable. "Just be yourself and express yourself," he advised her, "and keep on painting the way you like to paint, and what you like to paint, because what you like to paint pleases me much

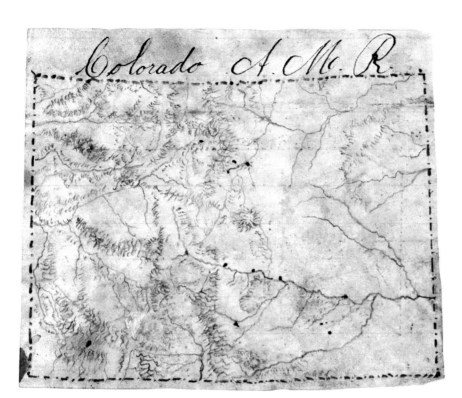

8. **Map of Colorado.** Circa 1870–80. Pencil on paper. Approximately 3¼″ x 4¼″.

9. Anna Mary Robertson at the age of eighteen. 1878.

more than most people, your own folks included, seem to realize. . . . Even if you do not do it for anyone else, I will be only too happy if you keep on painting just for me alone, for I always feel that sooner or later I will be able to publicly justify my opinion of you . . . and bring you some measure of respect and recognition for your efforts."[16]

Finally, in October of 1939, Caldor achieved his first success. "I have been persistently and patiently keeping after different people in the New York art galleries, and have not permitted myself to be discouraged by the many negative answers, excuses, and 'nos' that I have been receiving about your pictures," he wrote Moses.[17] "Well now my friends and all the others that poked fun at your self-taught 'homespun' style of painting will not make me feel bad any longer, as they

too often did. I have finally made good my promise to you and your folks that I would let no one discourage me, and keep at my efforts, no matter how long it would take me, to get others to appreciate your work as I understand it, when no one else took the trouble to encourage you."[18]

Caldor's jubilation was occasioned by Sidney Janis's decision to include three Moses paintings in a show of "Contemporary Unknown American Painters" that he was organizing for the Museum of Modern Art. However, the exhibition, which took place that fall in the museum's Members' Rooms, had little immediate impact on the artist's career because it was not open to the public. When it closed, the paintings were returned to Caldor, and Moses received a polite thank-you note from the museum. That was all.

New York, New York, Circa 1940

Interest in folk art—in the art of the untrained painter—was not new to sophisticated art circles in the autumn of 1939. The "Contemporary Unknowns" exhibition was, in fact, a follow-up to a much more significant show, "Masters of Popular Painting," that had taken place at the Museum of Modern Art the previous year. From its inception, the museum had been concerned with documenting the efforts of the self-taught, which, ever since the acceptance of Henri Rousseau (Plate 26) by Picasso and his circle, were seen as concomitants of the modern movement. After World War I, American artists returning from Europe had stimulated the collecting of nineteenth-century American folk art, and it was only natural that there should develop a heightened awareness of contemporary examples of the genre. The first such artist to receive public acclaim was probably John Kane (Plate 27), a Pittsburgh house painter whose artistic efforts were admitted to the Carnegie International in 1927. Horace Pippin, a black painter whose work was discovered in a shoemaker's window some ten years later, came to wider attention when four of his paintings were exhibited in the 1938 "Masters" show. It was within this context that Sidney Janis, who in 1942 would write the first American book on the subject,[19] developed his interest in locating native talent. Among those who debuted with Moses in his "Unknowns" exhibition was Morris Hirshfield (Plate 28), a retired garment worker later to be acknowledged, along with Kane, Moses, and Pippin, as one of the outstanding naïve painters of the twentieth century.

America was, in these years, a nation in search of an artistic identity. As art historian Barbara Rose put it, "Nearly two centuries after winning political independence from England, America was still an artistic colony of Europe. . . . American art did not achieve . . . maturity until the United States emerged as a dominant global power after World War II. Until that time, American artists continued to be torn between their allegiance to Europe's high culture and their wish to initiate a genuinely American style."[20]

To one recently come from Europe in 1939, American art was bound to appear distressingly provincial. Otto Kallir, a dealer in modern art who had fled to the United States after the Nazi takeover of his native Austria, was at once enthralled by the potential of his adopted homeland and appalled by what it offered artistically. Instead of the derivative art that filled the galleries on New York's Fifty-seventh Street, he longed to find an authentic American idiom. Like many proponents of the avant-garde, he shared an enthusiasm for folk art, and had on occasion exhibited it at his Vienna gallery. Now, what had been a secondary interest assumed primary importance. As soon as Kallir was able to obtain a car, he packed up his family and headed for the deserts of New Mexico and Arizona, where he knew he could find indigenous Pueblo and Navajo creations. Here, and not in the polished halls of Manhattan's art galleries and museums, he saw America's aesthetic promise fulfilled.

Back in New York, Kallir struggled to make known the pioneers of Austrian modernism—artists like Gustav Klimt, Oskar Kokoschka, and Egon Schiele—who are today, through his achievements, widely recognized but who were then virtually unheard of. His efforts soon became known to the rapidly growing refugee community in Manhattan. Thus it was that Caldor, himself by birth a citizen of the now dismantled Austro-Hungarian Empire, came to hear of Kallir's Galerie St. Etienne. He heard, furthermore, that Kallir was interested in the work of "primitive" or "naïve" artists, and so he repaired to the address given him by his informant.

Kallir, like Caldor, was a man who trusted his eye and made sure and spontaneous aesthetic judgments. He liked what Caldor showed him, he asked to see more, and he agreed to give the artist a one-woman show. Summer, the slow season in the art business, was quickly approaching, but he promised Caldor that he would hold the exhibition in the fall.

The exhibition, titled simply "What a Farm Wife Painted," may best be characterized as a modest success that had a surprising resonance. The short notices it received from most of the New York dailies tended to place the show within the burgeoning folk art trend. "The 'Primitive' which has been much to the fore . . . in the early season crops out again . . . at the Galerie St. Etienne," wrote *Times* critic Howard Devree.[21] Several papers printed lengthier, illustrated pieces, and *Time* magazine devoted two columns to the story. The exhibition was crowded, but of thirty-four paintings—reasonably priced at between twenty and two hundred and fifty dollars—only three sold.

10. **Bringing in the Maple Sugar.** 1939 or earlier. 14″ x 23″. (K. 42). This painting, one of the artist's earliest renditions of the "sugaring" scene, was included in her first one-woman exhibition.

A new dimension was given to Moses' reputation when Gimbels department store decided to reassemble the exhibition on its premises for a "Thanksgiving Festival." While previous write-ups had delivered straightforward accounts of the artist's life and discovery, Gimbels was prepared to hype the event for all it was worth. Ads called Grandma Moses "the white-haired girl of the U.S.A." and "the biggest artistic rave since Currier and Ives." But it was not the efforts of Gimbels' publicity department that charmed the hard-boiled New York City press, it was the presence of the artist herself. Grandma, who had declined to attend the St. Etienne show (Why bother, she said, since she had already seen the pictures anyway?), had been persuaded to come to New York and address the assembled multitudes at the Gimbels auditorium. "Grandma Moses Just Paints and Makes No Fuss About It" proclaimed one headline, almost in surprise. What did she think of her sudden fame? "Well, people tell me they're proud to be seen on the street with me," she replied. "But I just say, well, why weren't you proud to be seen with me before? If people want to make a fuss over me, I just let 'em, but I was the same person before as I am now."[22]

Grandma returned to Eagle Bridge and did not visit New York again for a number of years. Kallir sent her exhibition on to Washington, D.C., in early 1941, with less than encouraging results. Although the show received some good reviews, only one painting was sold. The purchaser was Duncan Phillips, who had long evidenced an astute eye in selecting works by American primitive artists. His museum, the first to acquire a painting by John Kane, now became the first to own a Grandma Moses.

From Amateur to Professional

Moses was beginning to be invited to enter her work in group exhibitions, and in 1941 her painting *Old Oaken Bucket* received a purchase prize from the Syracuse Museum of Fine Arts. Surprisingly, she was less than thrilled with her newfound status as an artist. "I have too much of it," she wrote Caldor in 1942, "have very little time to myself any more, have about made up my mind to go to my room and lock myself in and see no one. Every day or so there is a call for paintings, for an exhibit or to buy. They have had them in Washington, Albany, Fort Edward, Portsmouth, Syracuse, Hoosick Falls, Loomsack [*sic*—Walloomsac], Cambridge, Ithaca and now in Troy. All within nine months. Who could ask for more . . . ? Not I. I'd like to have a rest."[23] Moreover, she said of the exhibitions, "there was nothing in it but publicity, and I have got enough of that. My boys are so disgusted they threaten to bring suit if they could find out who wrote some of those articles that were in the papers. One of their neighbors asked if it was so that I could not read or write, being a primitive."[24]

For three years after her first one-woman show, Moses had very little direct contact with the Galerie St. Etienne. Kallir's initial arrangements had all been made with Caldor, who still considered himself the artist's agent even though she was freely selling to all who came her way. "I like to please everybody," she wrote Caldor two days after the St. Etienne show opened. "I'm trying to live up to my agreement, but the public are after me on all sides."[25] Moses resented the idea of being bound to any individual, be it Caldor or Kallir. Paintings, she thought, were not so different from butter or chickens. She set her price, sold them, and was satisfied. When Kallir resold the paintings for a higher amount and sent her a share of the profits, she was indignant and returned his check. Referring to Kallir, she wrote Caldor,

> I don't see how I can help him in any way more than to tell him not to ask such extortion prices for some of those shopworn paintings. He must come down on his prices or not sell.
> Now, it is this way, a man can bake a nice oven full of bread and pass it out to the public and tell them to eat all they can while it is good. Another man will take that bread and store it away in crocks, and it will get old and hard and stale, then nobody wants it. It is the same way with paintings. If I had to depend on pictures being sold that way, I would starve to death. I have paid my way through this world, ever since I was eleven years old, and I think I still can without outside help.[26]

Although aware that her art was becoming a marketable commodity, Moses still subordinated it to her farm chores. Old age had not in any way diminished her sense of responsibility or her matriarchal position in the family. "There is so much to do this time of year in the country," she wrote Caldor one spring, "and I still have to take the lead."[27]

Nevertheless, the publicity was beginning to alter her perception of herself as an artist. For one thing, it encouraged visits from a host of interested strangers. Eagle Bridge was on the map, and once there, a visitor could easily obtain directions to the Moses homestead from one of the locals. To New Yorkers vacationing in the Berkshires, the excursion was an interesting diversion. Grandma was a delight to talk to, and her paintings, priced at ten to fifty dollars, made unusual souvenirs and gifts. Cole Porter became accustomed to ordering a whole batch around Christmastime.

"We have talked about nothing else ever since [our visit]," a typical letter from a young actress begins. "Everyone is very envious of us having been with you, and our friend, Katharine Cornell, who has two of your paintings, calls up all the time to be sure I have not forgotten to tell her anything about you."[28] As did almost everyone who visited the artist, the actress ended her letter with a detailed list of paintings she wanted made to her order.

Inevitably, competition developed among the collectors vying for Moses' output. This centered, increasingly, on three people who demanded greater quantities of pictures than any of Grandma's other customers: Sidney Janis, who had kept in touch ever since the Museum of Modern Art exhibition; Ala Story, director of the American British Art Center; and Otto Kallir. Both Janis and Story endeavored to arrange exhibitions for Moses—Janis at other people's art galleries (he would later become a professional dealer) and Story at her own. Each of these three, aware of the other two, knew that Grandma, unable to fill all orders at once, was being forced to "play favorites." At one point, the artist issued specific instructions to Kallir: "If I should paint for you, you are not to let anyone know that I am painting for you, as it would make hard feelings. But you have ask[ed] me first, now keep *quiet*."[29] But, of course, if Moses took one customer's order out of turn, it was not long before the others were clamoring "take mine out of turn too."[30]

As time passed, and the orders for paintings continued, Moses realized a need to deal with her one-time hobby in a professional way.[31] The pressure of conflicting demands was only one of the difficulties she was experiencing in managing her own affairs. There was the very real problem of getting some purchasers to pay their bills. Also, as an artist in a rural backwater best reached by car, she found the market for her work at the mercy of the weather and, during the war, of gas rationing. In November 1944 Kallir and Story agreed to pool their efforts on Moses' behalf and pay her higher prices in exchange for a right of first refusal on everything she painted. Grandma accepted the arrangement without mincing any words: "It makes no difference to me for whom I paint, so if you and Mrs. Story can make a deal it will be all right."[32]

Grandma Moses' artistic career was born of two impulses—the appreciation of beauty and the need to do something useful—that stemmed from early childhood. Because her perceptions had always been conditioned by a sense of the aesthetic, she was able to incorporate painting in her daily routine without altering her basic attitudes. Art was a source of joy in the home, and a way to give enjoyment to others. Still, stern Puritan breeding made it impossible for Moses to condone any pursuit that was purely frivolous. A letter to her grandson indicates that she put practical considerations first: "As for myself, I shall continue painting. I can make more money that way, and it is easier for me than taking in summer boarders."[33] Yet she had no conception of the art market as such and was constantly baffled by the high prices her paintings could command. The significance of being able to sell her work lay not so much in its monetary implications as in the intangible rewards of having made a meaningful contribution. She expressed her attitude eloquently in her autobiography:

> If I didn't start painting I would have raised chickens. I could still do it now. I would never sit back in a rocking chair waiting for someone to help me. I have often said, before I would call for help from outsiders, I would rent a room in the city and give pancake suppers . . . I never dreamed that the pictures would bring in so much, and as for all that publicity, and as for the fame which came to Grandma so late, that I am too old to care for now.[34]

11. Letter from Anna Mary Robertson Moses to Otto Kallir. September 15, 1943. Here, shortly after Kallir's first visit to Eagle Bridge, Moses lays down the ground rules for their collaboration.

Fame

In 1944 Kallir held two Grandma Moses exhibitions at the Galerie St. Etienne, as if to make up for the fact that her paintings had not been shown there since 1940. Kallir's delay could in part be accounted for by his habit of testing and questioning his aesthetic judgments over a period of time. Moses' first work had been disconcertingly uneven in quality, a characteristic of many "primitives." However, her growing acceptance of her role as an artist had its counterpart in her art. She had begun to paint with greater assurance in these last years, venturing into freer compositions and larger canvases. Kallir was inclined to view her efforts with the increased seriousness necessary to make a prolonged commitment.

Otto Kallir was not a man given to aesthetic hyperbole, nor did he have many prestigious art world connections. When he gave Moses her first show, he was almost as much of a newcomer to New York City as she, and he barely knew English. His press releases were not masterpieces of sophistication. On the contrary, the release for the first exhibition, written by Caldor, contained such embarrassing analogies as, "Art, like murder, will sometimes out in the most unexpected places." By the second or third exhibition, Kallir had evolved a standard release that was nothing more than a condensed biography of the artist. Grandma Moses' extraordinary fame was kindled entirely by the simple facts of her life and the strength of her art.

There was something about Grandma Moses that moved people. The very fact that she was painting at all seemed a marvel: "a recipe for old-age deferred," one journalist called it.[35] Comedian Bob Hope, in his syndicated newspaper column, praised "the spirit that after ... years of battling the world was not content to ... rock itself away gazing backward but remained fresh enough to tackle something new."[36] Moses became "an inspiration to everyone who has always wanted to do something—whether it be writing or painting or studying music—and who has never found the time to do it."[37] Wrote another critic, "The homily for all to read is that it is not too late."[38]

Naturally, Moses was esteemed as a paragon by the aged, but others, too, found her example stimulating. "It takes a Grandma Moses to lift us out of our ruts, to make us understand the simple beauty which lies all about us in everyday living," stated one journalist.[39] Another agreed that she was "a reminder of the infinite possibilities of much we throw away in this world."[40] Yet a third thought she stood for "much that Americans believe in and hope for, but rarely find in American life."[41] "After a visit with Grandma Moses," declared a reporter who had just spent the afternoon in Eagle Bridge, "you feel better about art, America, the whole human race."[42]

Of far more significance than the analysis of the press was the response of the public. It was almost as though Moses' art had the power to heal; it became the repository of dreams. Unsuccessful artists found encouragement. "I had almost come to the conclusion that my art talent would have to be thrown aside," a woman from Tennessee wrote Grandma, "but ... having read about you has given me great courage—I shall always try to keep it up."[43] One man saw in Grandma's paintings nothing less than a panacea for the world's ills: "We are living in a pretty awful world, with war and disease and hunger and an atomic bomb," he commented. "The world that you show in your beautiful paintings ... is the kind of world we must try to bring back. Your pictures make people want that kind of a world, of a church, and a trout stream, and a barn, and cows, and children playing in the snow, and sugaring off in the maple sugar woods in March. When they see that kind of world they try to get it, so your pictures are not only beautiful and joyful to look at but are a good deal more than that."[44] Many told Moses that she had furnished them with strength to survive personal misfortune. "Dear Grandma," began a comment in the guestbook from one of her exhibitions,

> It gives me a great deal of joy and happiness. I was a mental patient. I am feeling fine now. Looking forward to a new life ... I feel I can do it and I will and must. When I know you did it. I feel I will also do it. You are my inspiration for life and love.[45]

Although the artist's personality was undeniably a factor in her appeal, it is important to note that she rarely appeared in public. She gave an occasional interview from her farmhouse in Eagle Bridge but had no intention of joining the New York City art whirl. What the public and the press saw were the pictures. In 1944 Kallir had launched a series of traveling exhibitions that, over the course of the next dozen years, made her paintings available in countless museums

12. Window display at Scribner's bookstore, New York City. 1952. Photograph by Otto Kallir. Grandma Moses drapery fabric, plates, reproductions and a record album, "The Grandma Moses Suite," are shown together with copies of the artist's autobiography and an original painting.

and small-town art associations nationwide. In 1946 he signed an agreement with the Brundage greeting card company that was destined to bring the art of Grandma Moses to an even wider audience. Brundage's announcement of a Moses Christmas "line" brought orders for sixteen million cards—four times the anticipated press run. That same year, the Dryden Press released the first book on the artist, *Grandma Moses, American Primitive*. The simultaneous publication of the cards and the book marked a turning point in Moses' career, catapulting her from local to national stature.

Grandma's new prominence was confirmed by the events of 1947. The book was reissued by Doubleday in a slightly expanded edition, and the greeting card license was taken over by Hallmark. For the first time, write-ups on the artist began to appear in the European press. The number of illustrated magazine pieces on her was increasing, as was the frequency of cover stories. Her eighty-seventh birthday in September was the first to be reported as a news event.

By the end of the decade, Grandma Moses was accepted as a national phenomenon. Not only was her birthday celebrated annually in the national news media, but she had become indisputably associated with certain traditional holidays. Thanksgiving and Christmas features on her work were standard practice. In 1949, when she traveled to Washington, D.C., to receive an award from President Truman, the press followed her every step of the way. Although five other women, among them Eleanor Roosevelt, also received awards, everyone agreed that Moses stole the show with what one reporter called her "genuine simplicity."[46] Truman, Moses said warmly, "is a country boy like my own boys," adding slyly, "I think he likes cows."[47]

If journalists were delighted that the artist's personality fully justified their expectations, Moses, for her part, was learning to handle the press with great aplomb and had overcome her original annoyance. "Why, those reporters were all right," she said, recalling her first real press conference. "You know how chickens come runnin' around when you go to the door to feed 'em? That's what those reporters made me think of. They were nice boys and girls."[48]

The name "Grandma Moses" was entering the vernacular. It was becoming a generic term connoting old age, unexpected talent, or potential realized. She had come to symbolize all amateur artists and was credited with initiating a boom in amateur art. In the mid-forties, advertisements for "how to paint" books had cleverly promoted their publications by suggesting that others try to paint like Grandma Moses. The idea caught on. Suddenly it seemed, in the words of one headline, as if "Everybody is Painting Now, and We Don't Mean Houses." The article went on to suggest that "women everywhere have the feeling that if Grandma Moses can paint, so can they.... [Art] is the only thing left...that is not mechanized, collectivized and regimented."[49] Another writer put it more bluntly: "To escape from the implications of a mechanistic age or...from the nightmare of atomic power...men and women all over the

U.S.A. are turning to painting."[50] There were other amateur artists of note—Churchill, Eisenhower—but somehow it seemed as if Grandma had started the ball rolling. Soon every homegrown artist of advanced years was being touted as "Grandma Smith" or "Grandpa Jones" or simply as "another Grandma Moses." But there never was another. If circumstance alone were responsible for Grandma's success, she did not have a monopoly on those circumstances. She did, nonetheless, have a monopoly on the success.

Through greeting cards, the national wire services, and illustrated periodicals, Grandma Moses was reaching a larger public than any living artist before her. She was, in many ways, on the technological frontier: one of the first artists to be discovered by the electronic news media. Via a complex telephone hookup, her voice was transmitted live from Eagle Bridge for a 1946 CBS radio broadcast. Her television debut two years later, in a program that combined filmed footage with live narration, was described as "an event unique in the history of radio and television."[51] This telecast was followed by a 1950 documentary on the artist, with narration by Archibald MacLeish, that was nominated for an Academy Award. Two years thereafter, in conjunction with the publication of her autobiography, *My Life's History*, Lillian Gish portrayed Moses in a televised dramatization. A then rare use of color on television was made to show Grandma's paintings in Edward R. Murrow's 1955 interview with the artist. It is interesting to note that this program was one of only two segments of the series "See It Now" for which CBS was able to obtain commercial sponsorship that year.

Each of the presentations in which Moses appeared before or spoke directly to the American public was compelling in its immediacy and authenticity. Though Grandma was by now accustomed to the repetition of routine questions, she was always capable of the unexpected. When Murrow, concluding his interview, asked her, "What are you going to do for the next twenty years?" he was a bit taken aback by her forthright answer. Pointing to the heavens, she said, "I am going up yonder. Naturally, naturally I should. After you get to be about so old you can't expect to go on much farther." Asked by Murrow whether she spent much time worrying about death, she quickly replied, "Oh no." Did she have any fear or apprehension about it? Again, "Oh no."[52] The interview was rebroadcast several times and was included in a memorial tribute to Murrow summarizing the high points of his career.

Grandma Moses and the Abstract Expressionists

Following World War II there was an accelerated desire on the part of Americans, whose culture had always been dependent on Europe's, to assume a leadership in the arts comparable to that attained in world affairs. An imitative art was no longer appropriate fodder for such ambition. Nor, in this era of mass communications, could a native idiom be expected to develop in isolation. The new American art would have to meet international standards, which meant, in effect, that it would have to meet European standards. Very naturally, Americans viewed their mission in terms of the modernist tradition as it had evolved in Europe earlier in the century. Their goal was to dominate that tradition by transcending it: to beat the Europeans at their own game. And when, after nearly two centuries of aesthetic obscurity, the United States finally came to the fore, it was considered nothing less than a victory. It is no accident that Irving Sandler's key study of the subject is titled *The Triumph of American Painting*.[53]

In view of America's cultural aspirations, Grandma Moses was seen as an embarrassment. When the U.S. Information Service sent a Moses show to six European capitals in 1950, protests rang out in American high art circles. Why wasn't American avant-garde art being sent abroad? But when, five years later, twenty-eight abstract expressionist works were shown in Paris's Musée National d'Art Moderne, the French response was disturbingly cool. The show, which included a cross section of the fine and applied arts compiled by the Museum of Modern Art, posed the old question, "Is there an American art?" "The overall average answer," reported *The New York Times* Paris correspondent, "seems to be—in painting and sculpture, no; in architecture, useful arts, photography, films and prints, . . . yes."[54]

By comparison, the Moses exhibitions were warmly applauded in the European press, much to the dismay of American critics. "Europeans like to think of Grandma Moses . . . as representative of American art," wrote a disgruntled reporter in *The New York Times*. "They praise our naïveté and integrity, . . . but they begrudge us a full, sophisticated artistic expression. Grandma Moses represents both what they expect of us and what they are willing to grant us."[55]

Actually, the American press misinterpreted the European bias. Europe saw America not as a land of country bumpkins, but as a technological fortress of skyscrapers, "Coca-Cola bottles,"[56] "rich snobs and eccentrics, highest living standards and top production figures."[57] The art of Grandma Moses came as a welcome surprise, not as confirmation of the expected. "Her radiant art disproves the stupid cliché that America has no soul," wrote one German paper. "Does it not speak very strangely in favor of America that this woman should have become so popular, even famous?"[58] Europeans were not clamoring for the new avant-garde art America longed to give them. They were happy to see, "in this age of aesthetic confusion," an artist who "has achieved clarity, . . . knows what she wants to do and . . . does it with a pure, deft technique." In the words of the British journal *Art News and Review*, "Grandma Moses' art is more likely to endure than the misshapen and demented ravings of the second generation of psychological and abstract painters."[59]

If it seems natural that Grandma Moses and the abstract expressionists were juxtaposed as representatives of opposite ends of the aesthetic spectrum, one must pause to remember that interest in naïve art had been initiated by the European avant-garde. Having thus paused, one can proceed to the conclusion that, whatever its origins, naïve art in the latter half of the twentieth century was not to occupy the lofty position decreed for it by the pioneer modernists. Abstract art had evolved in Europe from artists' desires to be free of the bonds imposed by the art academies. They therefore perceived the naïve artist, who lacked any sort of academic training, as a spiritual ally. It did not matter that naïve art was almost exclusively representational, for it occupied a realm entirely apart from academic realism. In America, which had historically lacked art academies in the European sense, a more restrictive conflict between abstraction and realism became the basis for much postwar aesthetic theorizing.

Americans, taking their cue from prewar European abstraction, more or less picked up where their foreign comrades had left off. As Sandler has pointed out, the approach that came to dominate American art criticism postulated a stylistic ascendancy "motivated primarily by formalist considerations" in which "advanced artists conceive new styles by rejecting recently established styles."[60] That is to say, in accordance with the governing critical perception, American art became progressively and deliberately more abstract. "Since resemblance to nature is at best superfluous and at worst distracting, it might as well be eliminated," decreed Alfred H. Barr, Jr., founding director of the Museum of Modern Art.[61]

As the abstract-realist dichotomy was inherent in the cultural climate of the era, it was only a matter of time before Grandma Moses became embroiled in the debate. Though Moses was hardly one to have strong opinions on aesthetic issues (she considered abstract art "good for a rug or piece of linoleum"[62]), her realism was perceived as an antidote to contemporary abstraction by the very people who promoted her. Otto Kallir was no fan of the American avant-garde. Because he had witnessed—nay, contributed to—the rise of modernism in Europe, he found America's attempt to emulate it redundant. When he wrote in *Grandma Moses, American Primitive* that Moses' paintings "have no connection with what we like to call 'the artistic expression of our time'; they are in fact the contrary of this art," he thought it was all to the good.[63] Louis Bromfield, writing the introduction to the same book, voiced similar sentiments.

People who found abstract art alienating rejoiced in the accessibility of Moses' paintings. "She dispels the myth that art is the province of the wealthy and the eccentric—it belongs to all of us," one reader wrote *Time* magazine.[64] Her paintings, agreed a critic, "talk, and they talk common sense. They breathe, and they breathe wholesomely."[65] Some mistakenly saw Moses' popularity as signaling the end of the era of abstraction. "The praise of the critics is encouraging," prophesied one New York daily, "for they should lead us out of the lanes of abstraction and intellectualized distortion."[66] Another columnist wrote with a down-home twang, "Grandma Moses, when she paints something, you know right away what it is—you don't need to cock your head sideways like when you look at some modern dauber's effort and try to deduct [*sic*] if it is maybe a fricassee of sick oyster or maybe an abscessed bicuspid or just a plain hole in the ground."[67]

As passionately as the intelligentsia wanted an American abstract art, the public did not want it. And, in all likelihood, if one took a survey of popular taste today, it would turn out that the majority still do not accept abstraction. "Ham and

14. The "Irascibles." 1950. Photograph by Nina Leen for *Life* magazine. *Top row (from left to right):* Willem de Kooning, Adolph Gottlieb, Ad Reinhardt, Hedda Sterne; *Middle row:* Richard Pousette-Dart, William Baziotes, Jimmy Ernst, Jackson Pollock, James Brooks, Clyfford Still, Robert Motherwell, Bradley Walker Tomlin; *Front row:* Theodoros Stamos, Barnett Newman, Mark Rothko.

13. Anna Mary Robertson Moses. September 1944. Photograph by Otto Kallir. Moses' rise to prominence occurred simultaneously with the rise of the American avant-garde.

eggs art," President Truman called it; "dribble art." It is an historical fact that the years when this controversy was brewing overlap exactly with the years in which Grandma Moses rose to fame. Some may call it a coincidence, others may see a cause for the latter in the former. In truth, like any simultaneous cultural occurrences, both the Moses phenomenon and the advent of abstract expressionism grew from their shared sociopolitical environment.

The years following World War II were pervaded by a sense of doom. The war, Sandler writes, "threw into sharp relief the dark side of man as inherent to his being; human irrationality could never again be dismissed as a passing aberration. The after-effects of the war—the possibility of atomic holocaust, the cold war—aggravated the anxious awareness of man's vulnerability and of his tragic condition."[68] Abstract expressionism, then, was in part a direct response to this existential uncertainty. Its mythos was a tragic one, fueled by the brutal circumstances under which several of its heroes perished. Young and vital artists such as Gorky, Rothko, and Pollock died tragically. Moses lived to be 101. She countered their pessimism with her optimism. She was the other side of the coin, the silver lining in the gray cloud. There was something almost miraculous, in these nervous times, about an old woman who could go on national television and say, in effect, "I am not afraid to die."

Grandma Moses' work was intrinsically concerned with mortality and immortality, both in fact and in implication. In fact, because it took for its subject matter the transient and enduring qualities of nature, and in implication because an artist as old as Grandma may die at any moment. Though her autobiography is full of anecdotes that illustrate the simple pleasures of country life, it is equally honest in its portrayal of its grimmer aspects. Anna Mary Robertson Moses, over ninety when the book was published, was a woman who had outlived most of her own generation, and many of her own children. Two of her brothers and one sister had died before reaching adulthood; half her children never lived beyond infancy. "We had to take the bitter with the sweet, always," she wrote. "Mother was very matter-of-fact, and she said, 'As you are born, you must die,' and Father took it in that way too."[69] With reference to her initial encounter with death, she recalled, "My worst memory goes back to the time when I first commenced to realize what the world was like, and I used to worry."[70] The artist had overcome such fears long ago.

"It's all set out," was the way Moses explained her philosophy of life. "There's nothing you can do about it. Just have faith, then you won't be wasting your years with worrying."[71] Hers was an ecumenical faith—a grandmother's wisdom, born of the no-nonsense advice that "worrying does no good." She had learned to accept death as one must on a farm, where the cycle of life is completed and repeated in endless variations. Moses was not offering an escape from the terrors of modern existence; rather, by her example, she provided people with the strength to endure.

Grandma Moses and the abstract expressionists were speaking to similar fears on the part of the American public, but the divergence of their methods and attitudes made them opposites. In intellectual circles, it increasingly seemed that despair and cynicism were the only rational responses to an age of irrationality. Thus, while Moses remained the darling of the popular press, she fell from favor with the critical elite. Meanwhile, the abstract expressionists, amidst a certain amount of philistine ridicule, gradually traveled from obscurity to prominence. Often cited as a milestone on this journey was the widely publicized protest of the so-called "Irascibles" (Plate 14) against a juried exhibition of contemporary art organized by the Metropolitan Museum of Art in 1950.[72] A sign of the turning tide, however, was the also well-publicized rejection of Moses' entry by the jury.

The Second Decade

The decade of the fifties saw ever increasing fame for Grandma Moses, coupled with growing antagonism. Though "primitive" art was in the final stages of being divorced from modernism, there were those who linked the two together in the "any child can do it" category. One wag delivered a catchy definition: "A primitive . . . is an artist who doesn't know much about painting, but knows what people like. Becoming a primitive is about the best thing an artist can do, ever since Grandma Moses made it popular. Not everybody can do it—you have to have a certain something. If you haven't, you may become an abstractionist."[73] The widespread aversion to "art talk" ("Art critics make with the words so deftly and insidiously that they can make people believe almost everything"[74]) was undeservedly applied to Moses. "We have always had a sneaking suspicion that her paintings caught on because [her] dealer pronounced them to be oracular utterances on the subject of rural life."[75] Cynics found it hard to believe that Grandma Moses could be a spontaneous phenomenon. If the facts did not support the contention that her fame was manufactured, journalists were not above rewriting the story. Why is Grandma Moses so famous? One clever fellow came up with an imaginative explanation: "The answer goes back to a bright winter morning some . . . years ago when a pair of eager young publicity men, temporarily unemployed and stranded in a small farm town, chanced to be walking down the street, wondering where their breakfast was coming from." The fictionalized account goes on to relate how the publicity men, after seeing Grandma's paintings in the drugstore, rush to sign her to a "hastily drawn contract" and then go "back to the big town with a great art 'discovery.'"[76]

If it is true that nothing succeeds like success, it is also true that nothing inspires resentment like it. "I was prejudiced by the furor over her, regarding it as a temporary excitement, a fad that would subside as others have," one journalist admitted.[77] Kallir, concerned that adverse criticism might upset Grandma, wrote to reassure her. "Mr. Kallir, Dear Friend," she replied,

Am so sorry you feel as you do about what people say.

15. **The Eisenhower Farm.** 1956. 16″ x 24″. The Dwight D. Eisenhower Library, Abilene, Kansas. (K. 1205).

This is a free country, and people will talk. Let them, if we do what is right they can't hurt us, and if one gets a little ahead of another then there is jealousy, always has been, always will be; and we must pay no attention to it, we must be *above* that. Now please don't worry about anything as far as I am concerned, for I am all right, have taken care of myself for the past ninety years and am good for another.[78]

One factor that fueled the growing controversy over the artist was the appearance of "Grandma Moses products" on the market. Was she being commercialized, people wondered? Her paintings were reproduced on drapery fabric, plates and wall murals, in small-format cards and larger sizes suitable for framing. Kallir, who cooperated with Moses in deciding which items to license, gradually established a set of ground rules to govern what constituted an acceptable use. Would her art be reproduced in accordance with the highest aesthetic and technological standards? Was the product something Moses herself might use? Nothing that was purely commercial was ever allowed. In principle, Kallir felt that the various Moses licenses were valid ways of making her art available to a greater number of people, not as substitutes for the actual paintings, but as supplements to them. He noted that such uses were being made of work by other well-known painters (Picasso is the example that springs most immediately to mind) whose art appealed to many more people than could afford originals.

From the very start, even before she began working

with Kallir, Moses had routinely retained the reproduction rights to her paintings when she sold or gave the originals away. Later, when the first requests for commercial licenses began to come in (for these inquiries were never solicited), Kallir took steps to safeguard the artist's oeuvre against unauthorized use. At a time when the procedure for copyrighting paintings was rarely utilized, he undertook to register all her work with the Copyright Office in Washington, D.C. To administer the copyrights and the payment of royalties to the artist, he founded a separate organization, Grandma Moses Properties. As a result, Moses' reproduction rights were more carefully policed and controlled than those of most other artists.

The availability of reproductions of the artist's work, initially inspired by popular demand, now had the reciprocal effect of increasing the public's awareness of her. It began to seem as if everything she did was a national news item. Her infrequent trips to New York—to speak before *The New York Herald Tribune* Forum in 1953, to attend an exhibition at IBM's Gallery of Arts and Sciences in 1955—were picked up by the wire services. There was increased interest in her daily routine. What time did she get up in the morning? What did she eat? Hundreds of papers nationwide were ready to spread the word if she sent President Eisenhower a message of encouragement or participated in the governor's program on aging. For many political hopefuls, shaking Grandma Moses' hand was as compulsory as kissing babies. The artist had been on the covers of *Time* and countless other national periodicals. In 1956, when Eisenhower's cabinet presented him with a specially commissioned Moses painting (Plate 15), the story made front pages across the country.

Grandma's birthday celebrations provide a sort of barometer of her fame. Her ninetieth, a landmark occasion in the life of any individual, was treated as one in the life of the nation. Grandma herself, however, was already looking forward to her hundredth. "I have invited a few of my friends over for a dance then," she said. Thereafter, her every birthday received national coverage and prompted numerous syndicated feature articles and editorials pointing out the positive values personified by the artist. As she approached the age of one hundred, the public marked each successive birthday with mounting anticipation, like the crowds in Times Square rhythmically counting down the seconds on New Year's Eve.

Grandma Moses' hundredth birthday was reported internationally as well as nationally. Noted photographer Cornell Capa was assigned to do a cover story for *Life* magazine. Sacks of congratulatory letters arrived daily for a week. "My, my, what a fuss they are making," said Grandma.[79] Former President Truman (who had sent greetings annually since their meeting in 1949), President Eisenhower, and Vice-President Nixon all paid tribute. Governor Rockefeller proclaimed the day, September 7, "Grandma Moses Day." The artist, as promised, got up and danced a brief, somewhat shaky jig with her physician, Dr. Clayton Shaw.

Moses, like any person her age, had had her bouts with sickness. Though she continued painting in her 101st year, her strength was failing. In May 1961 she took seriously ill, and after she recovered, she remained too weak to walk. Still, it was almost impossible for her family to keep her resting quietly in bed, for the artist had a desperate need to paint. "I got out my paintings t' finish up what I had, and I thought I wanted a tube of white lead," was the way Grandma explained one mishap. "I went about two steps to it, it was underneath the bureau, and I went down on my knees. . . . When I came to get up, I couldn't. Y' know, my feet dropped just like a dead duck's."[80] A series of such incidents convinced her family that Grandma Moses would be better off in a nursing home.

Grandma chafed against the restrictions imposed upon her in the local Health Center, where she was not permitted to paint and, for her own protection, was strapped into bed. She dreamed of being able to go home, of being able to paint again, but it seemed increasingly obvious that she never would. To avoid undue strain, preparations for her 101st birthday were kept to a minimum. Nevertheless, she was deluged by flowers and cards from all over the world. September 7 was another "Grandma Moses Day" in New York State that year. There were birthday greetings from a new President, John F. Kennedy, as well as from an old one, Harry Truman.

Approaching that birthday, Moses had remained alert and able to remember, with the lucidity often accorded the aged, the most vivid details of happenings decades back. Now, however, her mind began to wander more; she had moments of confusion and slept a great deal. In early October of 1961 Otto Kallir saw her for the last time. As he stood up to leave, she held out her hand to him, and he grasped it in

16. Grandma Moses on her 101st birthday. September 7, 1961. Photograph by Otto Kallir.

his. Never a woman given to long speeches or emotional displays, she said, quite simply, "Thank you." On December 13 he received a call from Dr. Shaw informing him that she had died.

Grandma Moses' death was front-page news in most of the nation's papers and, in the tabloids, was announced in the three-inch-high headlines usually reserved for murders and transit strikes. As the nation, led by President Kennedy, mourned her loss, the press took up the task of summarizing and evaluating her career. Journalists who had followed the rising value of her paintings over the years expressed a probing interest in the net worth of what they perceived as a "Grandma Moses empire." It had often been erroneously reported that she had earned a million dollars, a figure that amused her so much she inadvertently perpetuated the rumor by repeating it. Now, however, the silence of death was closing down on the Grandma Moses legend. Declared one headline, "Grandma's Wealth to Family; World Inherits Her Paintings."[81]

The Artistic Legacy

As the Grandma Moses legend had grown over the years, it had begun to feed off itself. Much of what was written about her—both positive and negative—was written not in response to actual contact with the artist, her paintings, or her writings, but in response to what others had already written about her. People reacted not to Grandma Moses the artist, but to Grandma Moses the artistic phenomenon.

The prevalence of reproductions that made Moses' work so well known had negative as well as positive effects. Prints and cards, which stressed the anecdotal rather than the painterly qualities of her art, misled those who had never seen an original. Reduced by a smaller format, the impact of her paintings was limited to its narrative aspect, which, in the tenor of the times, was too easily dismissed as "mere illustration." Indeed, many were inclined to see the artist as a designer of greeting cards rather than as a painter. As *New York Times* writer Harold Schonberg discovered, "No reproduction can begin to give the effect of one of Grandma Moses' representative paintings, with its remarkable depth, luminosity, richness of color and . . . composition."[82]

During the last decade of the artist's life, the split between her popular supporters and her intellectual detractors had widened. The fact that her work was deliberately being made available to people in all walks of life, through reproductions and related products, seemed to remove her from the more elitist realm of the "high" arts. Some thought that her great popularity, in and of itself, was proof of artistic mediocrity. André Malraux, in his epic survey of the arts, *The Voices of Silence*, expressed a widespread prejudice when he said, "It would be rash to assume that the emotions the modern crowd expects from art are necessarily profound ones; on the contrary, they are often superficial and puerile, and rarely go beyond a taste for violence, for religious or amatory sentimentalism, a spice of cruelty, collective vanity and sensuality."[83] Yet even if one accepts Malraux's premise, it would be unfair to conclude that, simply because the "crowd" is often attracted to the banal, everything it favors must be without merit.

For many, nevertheless, Moses' extreme fame overshadowed the genuine merits of her work. Critics were wary of her success. Her story was almost too well known: her old age, her sudden discovery, her homespun personality. Undeniably, she made good news copy. The question was, was she also a good artist?

The ruminations of Emily Genauer, art critic for two of the major New York dailies during the Moses decades, illustrate the effect that the artist's growing celebrity had on a certain segment of the press. Genauer had been shown Moses' work by Caldor in the days when he was still pounding the pavement with her canvases tucked under his arm. Through this circumstance, she became involved in the Moses saga even before it began. Later, she had occasion to recall that Caldor had offered to give her one of the then worthless paintings; she had, as a matter of principle, turned him down. But even back then, Genauer perceived a spark of quality in Moses' work. Her brief review of the first show at the Galerie St. Etienne was one of the most perceptive and therefore one of the most quoted. It was perhaps for this very reason that, as Grandma's renown began to spread, Genauer felt a need to reevaluate her initial impressions with some skepticism: "If you ask me whether this is important as art—which it certainly ought to be to merit such to-do—my answer must be an unequivocal 'no.'"[84] The question, however, continued to plague her. Moses' appeal "was a matter of taste and of very shrewd publicity," she mused a few years later, "but that can't be the whole story."[85] As the artist neared her last birthday, Genauer was still having trouble making up her mind. "Grandma Moses is a good painter," she declared, "although few, if any, of the pictures she has done to date are, by the friendliest estimate . . . works of art."[86] One may surmise that, while the critic was not satisfied with the inherent contradiction of this statement, she clearly felt ambivalent about endorsing such a highly publicized artistic sensation. Finally, she concluded that "not all the carefully maneuvered promotion in the world could have put Grandma Moses over, any more than it has succeeded in bringing fame to some other American Sunday painters favored by the attention of great museums and shrewd dealers. Grandma became world famous because her paintings were an affirmation of life in a time when the world was desperately seeking affirmation. They are witness that man, if he believes in something beyond himself, if he works tirelessly, if he learns with experience, can overcome great odds."[87]

But was this enough? Obviously, some did not think so. John Canaday, in his aesthetic postmortem for *The New York Times*, wrote, "Her magic was that she knew how magical it is to be alive, and in her painted records of her life she managed to relay some of that magic to the rest of us." Nonetheless, he contended that "her reputation was out of all proportion to her achievement."[88]

Not the least of the problems in evaluating Moses' achievement was that it flew in the face of the contemporary standards conceded to define good art. Formalist critics desired an abstract purism that left no room for realism of any sort, much less Grandma's. For those who held to an elitist view of culture, her mass appeal was anathema. Those too long steeped in the cynicism characteristic of much modern intellectual thought were appalled by her unabashed optimism.

In defiance of all these standards, the Moses phenomenon had lasted two decades. It had survived three presidencies, two wars, and instead of fading as fads do, often in a matter of months, only grew stronger with time. Why did the media not get bored with the endless repetition of the Moses tale? Why did the public not lose interest? The easy explanations frequently proposed—the artist's personality, her age, escapism, or nostalgia—cited factors that may have contributed to her appeal, but that in and of themselves could not have sustained it. The first two alone would have been insufficient, while the second two were irrelevant.

Very often, an artist's personality disappoints. Great painters are not always great human beings. Nevertheless, personal knowledge of an artist, his goals and philosophies, can shed light on his work. In the case of Grandma Moses, art and personality were complementary. People were pleasantly surprised, even thrilled, to realize that the woman was as unaffected as her paintings. Because she had the ability to express in words, through her interviews and her writings, the same impulses that were revealed more subtly in her art, the former became a meaningful adjunct to the latter. Her folksy story, her old age, served the function of underscoring these same impulses. She was all of one piece.

"Escapism" and "nostalgia" were handy labels used to dismiss the art itself. Neither quality, however, was to be found in her work. Moses was not preaching a return to the past, though she did paint partly from memories of a life that extended back into the previous century. The "old-fashioned" details in her pictures were, because of their stylistic simplicity, incapable of evoking the past in any but a symbolic sense. Her landscapes, on the other hand, were portrayed with an accuracy that was very much of the present. Ultimately, in both art and life, the forms of nature are the most enduring; they are eternal. There was a link between the present and the past in Moses' work that seemed to secure the future. The message was that some things—the scent of summer on the winds of spring, the bite of the first snow in November—do not change. She inspired not longing, but hope.

"What a strange thing is memory, and hope; one looks backward, the other forward. The one is of today, the other is the Tomorrow. Memory is history recorded in our brain; memory is a painter, it paints pictures of the past and of the day."[89] Thus Grandma Moses began her autobiography: lines so simple they verge on cliché. Yet these words are neither arbitrary nor simplistic. They convey the secret of Moses' achievement: memory and hope.

While formalism, elitism, and pessimism are qualities that have defined much twentieth-century art, they are not absolutes. There has historically been much art that aspires to realism, that is accessible and optimistic. The art of Grandma Moses is such an art. There is a point at which didactic rules must be abandoned and achievement measured as reflected in the work itself and the strength of its impact. Great art creates its own standards and can only be judged in terms of what it sets out to do. All art is in some very basic sense an affirmation of life; an offering of the human spirit —however downtrodden—as proof that the thoughts and feelings of mankind are ever precious and sometimes beautiful. Art, wrote Malraux, "is not a religion, but a faith. Not a sacrament, but the negation of a tainted world."[90] This, in essence, is the art of Grandma Moses.

17. **It Snows, Oh It Snows.** 1951. 24″ x 30″. Private collection. (K. 971).

CHAPTER TWO

FOLK ART IN AMERICA

What Is Folk Art?

The discovery of Grandma Moses would have been unthinkable had the stage not already been set by several decades of active interest in self-taught artists. She was initially taken up, not because she was exceptional, but because she conformed to a pattern typified by other painters of similar backgrounds. "'Primitive' painters have for three centuries created an original, independent kind of art for the American people, in an American idiom," wrote folk art expert Jean Lipman on the occasion of the artist's hundredth birthday. "Their work represents a continuous, vital, native tradition. In our time, this style has been personified by Grandma Moses who, famous and beloved at home and abroad, has herself become an American tradition."[91]

Yet, as Grandma Moses became a tradition unto herself, some started to feel that she should no longer be classified within the larger folk tradition. Fame had, for these observers, disqualified her. Certainly no folk artist before (or after) her ever achieved such widespread renown. Moreover, critics noted, success had caused the artist to abandon her amateur status, to turn pro, as it were. Was it permitted, they wondered, for a "Sunday painter" to paint Monday through Friday? Moses' painting style reflected her diligence; unlike that of other contemporary naïves, it developed and evolved. With time, her brushwork and handling of color became extraordinarily skilled and subtle. In the final years, Kallir himself contended that Moses was not really a primitive, but an impressionist. Or rather that her figures were primitive, but her landscapes were painted in an impressionistic manner.

The difficulty of classifying Moses' achievement was primarily engendered by a general inability to define "folk art." To this day, there is no single, coherent, universally accepted definition of the genre, nor can people agree on its importance relative to the "high" arts. Rather, there has been a tendency to adopt an "I-know-it-when-I-see-it" attitude, whereby creations are accepted and dismissed on the basis of personal rather than objective criteria.

The study of folk art is immature in comparison with academic art history. Originally proposed as a branch of ethnology or anthropology, it is still not accepted in the curriculums of most university art departments. Primitive or naïve art was dragged into the realm of the fine arts by the artists themselves—by postimpressionists such as Gauguin, by the cubists Braque and Picasso, by Kandinsky, by expressionists such as Oskar Kokoschka, and even by the abstract expressionists Pollock, Rothko, Gottlieb, and Newman. This interest on the part of three successive generations of the avant-garde was enough to vouchsafe "primitivism" a place in the footnotes of modernist history. It was not quite enough to make it a discipline in its own right.

Because folk forms, until the twentieth century, were relatively unrecorded, historians had to start from scratch in researching the field at the very moment when socioeconomic changes were wiping out some of its older traces. It took decades merely to reconstruct a semblance of an historical record, let alone to arrive at theoretical or qualitative judgments. Naturally, initial efforts had to concentrate on the former with only cursory attention to the latter.

The problem of defining folk art plagued scholars from

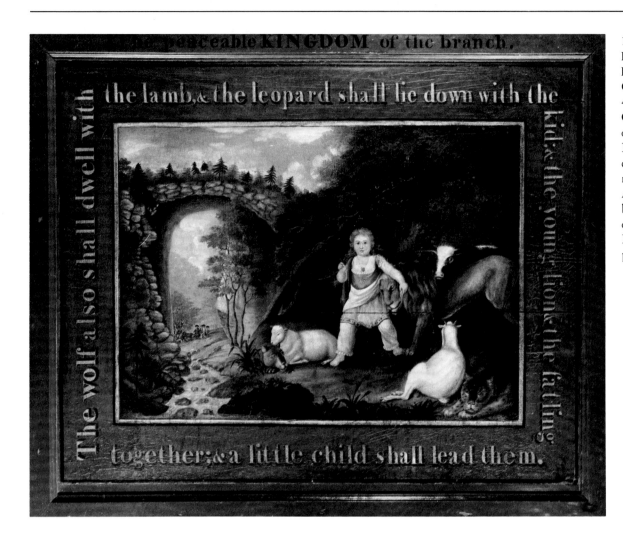

The painting within the frame bears the text:

peaceable KINGDOM of the branch,

the lamb,& the leopard shall lie down with the

kid:& the young lion:& the fatling

The wolf also shall dwell with

together:&a little child shall lead them.

18. Edward Hicks. **The Peaceable Kingdom of the Branch.** Circa 1825–30. Oil on wood. 36¼″ x 44⅞″. Yale University Art Gallery, New Haven; Gift of Robert W. Carle. Hicks, generally considered the greatest nineteenth-century American folk painter, based his famous depictions of the "Peaceable Kingdom" on popular prints (Plates 19 and 20).

the start, not the least because they desired some ground rules for their efforts. Increasingly it seemed that they were grappling with a multilimbed animal ready to throttle them with an unseen arm just when they thought they had gotten all the legs pinned down. What was folk art anyway? African tribal masks? Native paintings from the Caribbean? Naïve paintings from Europe in the manner of Henri Rousseau? The jottings of raving lunatics? Of children? Was it the anonymous votive offerings found in wayside chapels? The carved and painted wardrobes of Eastern Europe? The many and sundry handmade items of beauty and charm—buttons, pipes, shepherds' crooks, weathervanes, wallpaper, crockery, toys, quilts, ad infinitum—that graced common homes from Bosnia to California in the centuries before mass-produced goods became the norm? Was it the professional limner portraits of America, the decorative daubings of signmakers and wall painters, of housewives and schoolchildren, bored aristocrats and industrious farmers? The very fact that the genre went by such a diversity of names—

"folk," "primitive," and "naïve" being the most frequent—was symptomatic of its identity crisis.

Folk art is, in fact, everything that everybody always thought was *not* art before the modernist revolution at the turn of the century.[92] Even today, the arguments persist as to whether the "folk" or the "art" should be deemed the crucial element. Folk art is a catchall category for any art created outside the European academic tradition; "nonacademic" is actually a better word for it. This rather unwieldy agglomeration is composed of a number of distinct and cohesive traditions each deserving of study in its own right. Works created by societies that had only passing contact with what is pompously called "Western civilization" must be kept separate from European-influenced artifacts. Works by amateurs should not be confused with those of professionals, and in the amateur class, the creations of children and the emotionally disturbed (who are handicapped by more than just lack of training) have to be dealt with differently. Within

19. H. S. Tanner. **A Map of North America.** Engraving. Published in Philadelphia in 1822. The Library of Congress, Washington, D.C.

20. Richard Westall (after). **The Peaceable Kingdom of the Branch.** Engraving. Published in London in 1815. Rare Book Department, The Free Library of Philadelphia.

the European sphere of influence, it must be recognized that crafts objects and paintings encompass two distinct traditions, and should be treated as such even (perhaps especially) when they overlap. Many problems of definition are created by scholars who inadvertently attempt to exclude one or another of these categories from their overall conception of the field or, alternatively, who have tried to explore them all simultaneously.

One of the gravest pitfalls confronting the student of folk art is the temptation to formulate comprehensive stylistic guidelines. "Folk" is not a style in the sense, say, that cubism or impressionism are styles. It refers to the circumstances under which art is created rather than to the art itself. The adjectives often used to describe it—awkward, primitive, naïve, fresh, direct—are indicative of subjective evaluations rather than objective standards. One may follow each of the adjectives with the query "In comparison to what?" and the answer will always be the same: "Academic European art." Visually, there are no overriding similarities to unite all

works of nonacademic art beyond those that distinguish them from academic art: lack of correct perspective, lack of flawless three-dimensional modeling, and so on. While certain groups of folk objects do display internal stylistic cohesiveness traceable to a shared craft heritage or outside influences, these particular attributes are not transferable to the field as a whole.

Another common fallacy is the notion that true folk art is uninfluenced. No art is created in a vacuum; art cannot spring from nowhere full-blown, like the goddess Athena from the head of Zeus. Folk artists, like all artists, have been highly sensitive to visual stimuli in their environments, and almost none was completely isolated. However, the academic forms that came their way were adapted to their individualistic purposes, rather than vice versa, as can happen in an art academy. Consequently, the best folk painters created unique styles that were amalgams of outside source materials, personal motivation, and whatever rudimentary technical skills they could acquire.

American Primitive (Professional)

The work of Grandma Moses belongs in the American substratum of the European tradition that might best be termed professional nonacademic painting. America, by the early nineteenth century, had a well-developed class of such artists. They served the needs of a public too geographically and culturally remote from Europe's fine art market to participate in it. Theirs was an ad hoc art. Limners, as these often itinerant professionals were called, would have painted according to the latest European style if only they could have obtained the training to do so. Instead they studied sporadically with those individuals blessed by the academic experience, they taught each other, or they taught themselves. Through this network of personal instruction and through how-to manuals and imported mezzotints and engravings, an awareness of academic conventions was transmitted to the United States.

The American professional nonacademic painter had recourse to two historical sources: the post-Renaissance tradition of easel painting and a craft system derived from the medieval guilds. In the Middle Ages, no distinction was made between crafts and the so-called "high" arts. Later, the old customs governing the production of utilitarian objects became the basis for Europe's folk culture, while the aristocracy and the academies supported a more refined aesthetic. The American folk painter made use of both traditions to a greater or lesser extent in accordance with his inclinations and circumstances. As such, he was neither fish nor fowl, neither pure craftsman nor true high artist, but a curious composite of the two.

Professional status gave artists more opportunity to grow and experiment than amateurs usually gave themselves. As more extensive oeuvres are attributed to recognized artists, it becomes readily apparent that nonacademics evidenced the same sort of stylistic evolution seen in the work of practicing academicians. There is a point at which the two categories begin to overlap, as in the early, "primitive" work

21. Samuel F. B. Morse. **Portrait of Lucretia Walker Morse.** Circa 1822. Oil on canvas. 30″ x 25″. Amherst College, Mead Art Museum; Gift of Herbert L. Pratt.

of artists like Benjamin West, who eventually obtained training in Europe, or the later work of "primitives" like Edward Hicks, who displayed a remarkable degree of technical finesse. Many portrait limners embodied the academic and the nonacademic concurrently, executing deftly modeled faces but unconvincing hands and stylized drapery.

Evidence clearly suggests that the professional nonacademic chose his career deliberately and at an early age. Often fine arts and crafts elements mingled in the vocation. Sign painters, coach painters, and other craftsmen found their training suited them equally to fine art commissions, which provided welcome supplements to their incomes. Some switched over entirely to this kind of work, while others alternated between the two. One of the more remarkable artists to develop from a crafts background was the Quaker preacher Edward Hicks. Trained as a coach painter,

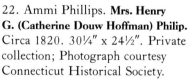

22. Ammi Phillips. **Mrs. Henry G. (Catherine Douw Hoffman) Philip.** Circa 1820. 30¼" x 24½". Private collection; Photograph courtesy Connecticut Historical Society.

and motivated by profound religious fervor, he transformed images derived from prints (Plates 19 and 20) into some of the most forcefully original American paintings of his century (Plate 18).

Some nonacademics never dabbled in the crafts. Ammi Phillips (Plate 22) is one of the better-known artists who seem to have applied their talents almost exclusively to the fine arts. It is not known what, if any, training he may have obtained, though it is clear that in his lengthy and prosperous career he passed through several stylistic phases, each of which may be connected with the influence of a fellow limner. A comparison of his work with that of academic painter Samuel F. B. Morse (Plate 21) shows that Phillips was not at all unfamiliar with the basic tenets of European portraiture. It was in the area of improvisation, rather than innovation, that such limners revealed their greatest skills.

America Comes of Age

It is often said that the American folk tradition reached its zenith in the nineteenth century. Certainly the times were ripe for it. There was sufficient cultural distance from Europe as the first generation born in the newly created nation came of age, and sufficient leisure and economic stability as the colonial settlements took root. The War of 1812, sometimes called the second war of independence, provoked a surge of patriotic pride. This chauvinistic spirit, which touched every aspect of American life, prompted a desire for a national art. The age of Jacksonian democracy further confirmed the egalitarian notion that art, like government, should be by the people and for the people.

Jacksonian Americans let loose that now all-too-familiar battle cry: "Give us an art we can call our own!" They charged into the fray, burdened with the same inconsistencies that have since handicapped Americans in that endless struggle. They wanted a national art, yes. But as was natural for a people of predominantly European origin, they wanted to define it in terms of European standards. The fledgling American art academies, often little more than fraternal organizations for artists, served as conduits for European culture. European-trained artists taught there; talented American pupils were winnowed out and sent across the Atlantic to seek their destinies.

Art historians have long tried to distill the quintessentially American qualities that Americans, under these circumstances, brought to their art. Quite clearly, one of their most unique assets was the American landscape itself— a landscape that was even sought out by Europeans as an example of primeval wilderness, a variety of exotica. Thus there arose a native landscape tradition, first in the meticulously detailed lyricism of the Hudson River School, and later in the more atmospheric portrayals of the luminists. Genre scenes depicting typically American vignettes were another art form that, simply by dint of subject matter, could not be duplicated abroad. Stylistically, however, both types of painting displayed a direct derivation from the European: from the landscape tradition of Claude Lorrain, from the obsessive realism of the Düsseldorf school, from the Pre-Raphaelites, the romanticism of Caspar David Friedrich, and the proto-impressionism of Turner.

The position of landscape in American folk art is hard to assess. Confined to the forbidden category of frivolous decorative art by the Puritans, it only became more common when the religious doctrine was relaxed in the mid-eighteenth century. Nonetheless, much professional work continued to revolve around portraiture. If one considers that many seeming landscapes were actually also portraits of a sort—of ships, of farms—the proportion of portraits to landscapes becomes even greater. While high artists were concerned with the romance of the American wilderness, the folk artist was more interested in recording its conquest. Artists like Thomas Cole took an early environmentalist stance favoring the preservation of the natural scene, but folk painters concentrated on the man-made contributions to that scene.[93] Since the development of any sort of native landscape art was relatively recent, it may be that, true to a generally observed pattern, the innovations begun in the academic arts in the 1820s and '30s did not filter down to the folk arts for another generation or so. When they did, their acceptance was fostered by a number of interrelated cultural developments.

At mid-century, the era of the portrait limner was grinding to a halt with amazing rapidity. The introduction and growing popularity of the daguerreotype effectively eliminated the market for the more costly oil portrait. Many folk painters were forced to look for new subject matter. It is not surprising that young artists like George Henry Durrie (Plate 34), who had trained to become portrait limners, turned to landscape instead. They had before them as models the members of the by now established Hudson River School, whose work could be seen in recently founded museums and in lithographic reproductions. Lithographs provided an important source of imagery for the folk artist, as well as a different outlet for his own endeavors. Durrie, who struggled in vain to make it as a member of the high art crowd, instead achieved undreamed of popularity under the auspices of Currier and Ives. His characteristic combination of landscape and genre was a little too polished to be truly primitive, and a little too folksy to be academic. His success points up the intrinsic connection between folk and mass culture.

23. Fanny Palmer (after). **The Old Oaken Bucket.** 1864. Lithograph. Published by Currier and Ives, New York. The Harry T. Peters Collection; Museum of the City of New York. The popularization of landscape lithographs prompted folk painters to try their hands at the genre (Plate 24). Grandma Moses would later paint numerous versions of "The Old Oaken Bucket" (Plates 54 and 57).

By the second half of the nineteenth century, mass production had entered the arts, vastly increasing the amount of visual material available to the general public. Engraving and its offshoots—etching, aquatint, and mezzotint—were long-established forms of low-budget art. Now, however, newly invented printmaking media, the advent of more efficient paper production, and power presses made high-quantity printing practical for the first time. Wood engraving, which permitted the simultaneous reproduction of images and type, facilitated the creation of illustrated periodicals. Lithography, a German invention that surfaced in the United States in the 1820s, offered a cheaper alternative to intaglio. The new art reproductions were complemented by a host of clever marketing schemes designed to reach a newer, wider audience.

Aesthetically, lithography was fueled by various elements of the American tradition. Many prints were copies of

24. C. W. Clapp. **Old Oaken Bucket.** Circa 1880. Oil on canvas. 34″ x 43¼″. Kennedy Galleries, Inc., New York.

recognized academic works, but many were copies of paintings made specifically for the lithograph trade. In the latter, selected mannerisms and subjects of the high artist emerged transformed. By nature a popular art form, lithography had a tendency to turn culture into kitsch, to emphasize subject matter over style, accessibility over the aesthetic. Thus it is that early lithography is remembered more for its tawdry than its exalted moments—for garish colors rather than subtle harmonies and for sentimental genre scenes rather than the faithful evocation of pure landscape. Its great asset was flexibility, the ability to serve both advertising and art, to attract the largest public with a diverse presentation of goods. Those who look for evidence of a lowest common denominator will find it in the scores of sheets illustrating darky jokes, sensationalizing human tragedies, or coyly idealizing young love.

That democracy contained a threat as well as a promise, something known to the founding fathers of the United States and seemingly forgotten in the era of Jacksonian patriotism, was a notion that acquired new significance when the technological revolution brought about democratization to an extent never before envisaged. Peter C. Marzio, who writes eloquently in defense of the much-maligned chromolithograph, points out that by the end of the nineteenth century, these prints had come to symbolize the destruction of civilization itself.[94] One critic claimed that the proliferation of lithographic art created a "pseudo-culture" in which the taste of the presumably tasteless masses replaced loftier standards: "A society of ignoramuses who know they are ignoramuses might lead a tolerably happy and useful existence, but a society of ignoramuses, each of whom thinks he is a Solon, would be an approach to Bedlam let loose."[95]

The United States would enter the twentieth century without having achieved a national art of international resonance. The American artist-in-exile might be absorbed by the European mainstream; the reverse had not come to pass. Ironically, it was in the area of the disgraced popular arts that Americans made the first inroads toward a distinctive culture: not just in prints and magazines, but later in music, radio, movies, and television. These, however, because of their broad-based support, were perceived as a challenge to the European system, which was by nature elitist. Americans were wont to look upon their accomplishments in the area of mass art with little respect, let alone pride. It has taken us many decades to forgive the pioneers of

chromolithography and to realize that film, for instance, can attain the level of a high art. (We are not yet ready to accord similar status to its lowly offspring, television.)

The "people" (or folk) had always had their own art, an art different from that endorsed by the elite. In the twentieth century, the role once occupied by folk art—a substitute aesthetic for the lower classes—was taken over by the mass media. Where once there had been two cultural strands, academic and nonacademic, now there were three. The third was technological in its orientation and "popular" in a way lower-volume handcrafted art could never hope to be. These cultural changes, of course, had explicit economic overtones. Mass production soon outmoded both the craftsman and the folk painter.

Seemingly doomed by the virtual elimination of its popular patronage, folk art suddenly acquired aesthetic cachet in elitist circles. It would have surprised earlier folk artists to see their creations, having survived their original public, granted a second life as the playthings of the twentieth-century avant-garde. The dream of the pioneering European modernists, academic by training but not by inclination, was to become nonacademic. Folk artists, who had done this of necessity rather than by choice, were an inspiration.

America inherited an awareness of folk art along with all the other cultural baggage of the European avant-garde. In America, however, two factors that had provided a critical rationale for the Europeans were lacking: a pervasive academic structure and a profound contempt born of forced intimacy with same. Moreover, Americans acquired their interest in nonacademic art secondhand and a little bit after the fact. By the time they caught on, in the period between the two world wars, the modern movement had passed out of its early, revolutionary stage. No longer crucial as confirmation of the instincts of aesthetic rebels, folk expression had lost its ideological edge. Thus, America's discovery of nonacademic art never had the same urgency as Europe's. By the 1940s the field was unenthusiastically accepted as a "mildly amusing bypath of art called 'Primitive Lane.'"[96]

Americans greeted the new interest in folk creations with pronounced ambivalence. The genre embodied all the conflicts that would condition their reception of Grandma Moses: it was essentially popular rather than elitist, realist rather than abstract, provincial rather than cosmopolitan. By definition an art of the people, folk art would lose prestige if viewed as an art of the masses. Yet there was no escaping the fact that folk painting provided a representational alternative for the many who were alienated by abstraction. Americans could not forget that their folk tradition had once been scorned as an inept emulation of European academicism. Its reappraisal in accordance with the philosophies of Europe's new avant-garde was heartening, but no substitute for a mature, sophisticated national art. There remained a sneaking suspicion that training *does* count for something, that the achievements of the self-taught are only remarkable in the light of their limitations, and not in and of themselves. Even Holger Cahill, a pioneering folk art advocate, conceded that "[such works] cannot be valued as highly as the work of our greatest painters and sculptors."[97] Twentieth-century folk art, especially, was challenged on all sides. Some discounted it altogether, insisting that no valid folk art can be created in the technological age. Others deplored the depressing lack of standards in a field that disowned the usual academic rules governing quality. "Though a flood of pictures is being created by a virtual army of contemporary naïve painters, only a handful possess the talent to create pictures that will stand the test of time," admitted Robert Bishop, one of the most outspoken champions of modern folk art.[98]

Today, contemporary nonacademic painting has become boxed in by the pressures of the commercial marketplace, on the one hand, and the indifference of the critical establishment, on the other. Popularization has encouraged a plethora of pseudo-naïves, whose very existence serves to discredit the genuine exponents of the genre. Actually, folk art has changed very little, intrinsically. The academic and crafts systems that provided its historical reference points are gone, of course. Art schools still exist, but now they preach the tenets of the avant-garde. The crafts structure has been dismantled and replaced by a pervasive combination of technological mass arts. Folk painters remain outcasts who work outside these established systems, drawing from one or the other without being absorbed by the traditions that spawned them. Like their predecessors, they may have some training, but not enough to convert them to any preexisting style. The majority of their efforts are inept, imitative, dull. The gifted few, however, are able to extract from their models those aspects best suited to their personal expressive needs and combine them with gradually perfected technical skills in an inventive manner. In this, they still exemplify the ideal of individually created style and total aesthetic freedom postulated by the pioneers of the European avant-garde.

Grandma's Contemporaries

Early twentieth-century nonacademic artists were likely to be amateurs. The same forces that had undermined the market of the professional in the previous decades stimulated the output of the amateur. Photography, lithography, illustrated periodicals—the flood of images inundating the country increased the desire for art and prompted the idler to occupy his leisure time with brush in hand. Access to original paintings was improved after the first major American museums were founded in the 1870s. Education was becoming more widespread, and art training was often incorporated in the curriculum. Statistics show that as the number of limners declined, the number of art supply stores serving the general public multiplied.[99]

European amateur artists of the late nineteenth and early twentieth centuries generally strove to emulate the work of (often conservative) academic masters. Henri Rousseau (Plate 26), when he gave up his post as a municipal toll collector in Paris, followed the established customs of would-be artists: he applied for permission to copy at the Louvre and joined the official Salon. His idols were Gérôme, Clément, and Bouguereau. Only when the Salon would not exhibit his works did he join the more progressive Société des Artistes Indépendants, whose number included Seurat and Signac. Louis Vivin, also a retired French civil servant, was inspired to pursue his artistic inclinations because the academic artist Meissonier appeared in a dream to inform him that he had the makings of a great painter.[100]

American amateurs tended to align themselves with a more populist tradition, to paint simply for pleasure rather than to nurture lofty ambitions. Many who grew up in the latter half of the nineteenth century shared vestiges of the craft system that had fostered their professional predecessors. Joseph Pickett, for example, began by decorating the carnival concessions he ran. John Kane (Plate 27) was painting boxcars when he thought to turn his brush to more expressive use.

Artists who painted from a craft background usually

25. Photograph of the Juniet family and their cart. Courtesy James Johnson Sweeney. Though it is known that Henri Rousseau copied printed and photographic images, for many years this snapshot was one of his few published sources.

approached the occupation in terms of "how" rather than "why." Jean Lipman noted with interest that the nineteenth-century artist Rufus Porter (Plate 32), writing a manual on mural painting, began with technical, not aesthetic, advice: "Dissolve half a pound of glue in a gallon of water, and with this sizing, mix whatever colours may be required for the work . . . "[101] Similarly, Moses answered the question, "How do I paint?" with the explanation, "Well, first I get a frame. Then I saw my Masonite board to fit the frame. Then I go over the board with oil, then give the board three coats of flat white paint."[102] These artists were precise and professional about their work. "I love to take my time

and finish things up right," wrote Moses.[103] John Kane agreed: "I take pains with my work. One thing I cannot abide is sloppy work in any form. I think a painting has to be as exact as a joist or a mold or any other part of building construction."[104]

In America, land of opportunity, there was a sense that art, no less than anything else, was a field open to everyone. "Anybody can paint if they go about it," Grandma Moses often said. "Could you sweep this floor?" she asked a reporter, hurling the question with such vehemence that the woman almost jumped out of her chair. "You could. But you'd have to get about doing it. That's how it is with

26. Henri Rousseau. **The Cart of Père Juniet.** 1908. Oil on canvas. 38¼″ x 50¾″. Musée de l'Orangerie; Collection Walter Guillaume. Photograph courtesy Musées Nationaux, Paris.

paintin'."[105] Porter's instructional essays were based on the same premise. He voiced the then unheard-of opinion that "it is not infrequently the case that the productions of self-taught artists far surpass in excellence those of regular bred artists."[106]

Often neglected in studies of American folk art is the impact of the pioneer spirit of adventure and inventiveness. It is no accident that Porter—artist, teacher, and writer—also founded the *Scientific American* and formulated prototypes for an automobile, an airplane, and an elevated railroad. Nor is it a coincidence that Moses and Caldor corresponded about ideas for patents—her fabrication of a

rubber-clad dishrack, his creation of a new kind of percolator—or that Otto Kallir was an avid follower of the early history of aviation. This was the ideal—that all things are possible and that progress is good—that moved America on into the twentieth century. Art was one component of the American dream.

For many years, however, it was a dream unfulfilled, the pursuit of which had to be its own reward. When Pickett died, his few surviving works were bought in at the estate auction arranged by his wife. Two paintings that Kane donated to a convent were relegated to the basement "to scare

27. John Kane. **Prosperity's Increase.** 1933. Oil on canvas. 31½″ x 39½″. Collection William S. Paley.

away the rats."[107] It is not surprising that the first generation of American amateurs to receive public recognition initially thought of painting as no more than a pleasant pastime; they had little hope of selling their creations. These artists, of whom the best known today are Kane, Pippin, Hirshfield, and Moses, all grew up in the late nineteenth century, when professional opportunities for the self-taught were at an ebb. Each only began painting seriously after age or infirmity had denied him other work. They thus were inclined to consider art a mere substitute for more "practical" labor. "I wouldn't want anyone to think that I gave up outdoor painting when I was recognized as an artist," Kane was quick to explain. "I gave it up when I could no longer get it."[108]

It is understandable that these painters saw their artistic careers, accurately, as relatively minor in proportion to the rest of their lives. As has often been noted, Moses devoted the bulk of her autobiography to her childhood and married life, and only a small fraction to her later accomplishments. Likewise, the autobiographical sketch of Horace Pippin, a wounded ex-soldier, focuses on his war experiences; he includes one sentence on his painting: "One day I decided to get some oil paint, and I started a picture that was in my mind... and made others until my work was discovered."[109]

Most amateurs were unencumbered by an overriding awareness of the distinctions that separate high and low art. The most unlikely images appealed to them, and they had no qualms about incorporating them in their work. Pippin's earliest paintings were probably copied from old prints and life insurance calendars. Morris Hirshfield, who became a painter after ill-health forced him to give up his business, sought out a cheap colored lithograph (Plate 29) to use as a model for his painting of a lion (Plate 28). Before embarking on a new subject, he often asked his advisor, Sidney Janis, to assemble files of photographs.[110] Hirshfield's first painting had actually been a reworking of someone else's canvas; the artist applied his characteristic rich textures to a preexisting composition, leaving just one segment of the original exposed. Similarly, John Kane, during slack periods in the construction industry that provided his primary source of income, peddled overpainted photographic enlargements door-to-door. Years later, when some of these found their way into an exhibition, they created a scandal that baffled the artist.

As folk artists began to be encouraged by the cultural elite, their reliance on printed or photographic sources was treated like an embarrassing secret. The fact that nearly all such artists, including ones so illustrious as Edward Hicks and Henri Rousseau (Plates 18 and 26), copied other images to some extent, contradicted the prevalent myth that genuine naïve art is uninfluenced. For a long time, myth was stronger than truth. It is only recently that the academic and popular origins of nonacademic art have been objectively studied, thus making it possible to establish its art historical context.

Meanwhile, self-taught artists were taken in hand by their mentors and told to stop copying. "It makes no difference how well an artist paints today, the important thing is to be original," Caldor scolded Moses in 1939. "You have no idea how upset I was... when someone whom I expected real help from in my plans came up to look at your pictures and became very sarcastic... I was never so humiliated and disgraced in all my life. Imagine me insisting that, as far as I knew, the pictures were your own idea, and then having this fellow invite me to a nearby bookstore and showing me the very same thing in one of the most popular artbooks being sold today."[111]

Books and prints and photographs, for the self-taught, took the place of art schools. And just as painters through the ages have learned by copying the works of those who came before them, so the nonacademic artist learned, free-style, from these materials. John Kane, whose first two entries to the Carnegie International had been rejected because they were copies, took a firm stand in favor of artists employing such methods: "All artists, no matter who, are copying nature.... If an artist sees something in a book he likes, he will copy that, too, enlarging upon it or lessening it according to his requirements. So it makes no difference where he sees it, whether it is the work of nature or of another man or work in a book. He is bound to react to the inspiration he feels. He will copy in part, and adapt and take out what he likes."[112]

K ane lived to see his work accepted by the Carnegie International, and other exhibitions followed. Nonetheless, within seven years of this first breakthrough, he died in the slum tenement he had occupied before. Pippin at least managed to reap some financial reward from his art, but he passed away nine years after his first one-man show. Hirshfield was accorded the honor of a retrospective at the Museum of Modern Art only four years after his first

28. Morris Hirshfield. **Lion.** 1939. Oil on canvas. 28¼″ x 40¼″. The Sidney and Harriet Janis Collection; Gift to The Museum of Modern Art, New York.

showing. He died three years thereafter.

Kane, Pippin, and Hirshfield did not live to cope with the growing market for their work. That they all hovered somewhere between amateur and professional status is attested to by the relatively small size of their oeuvres (on the average, between 60 and 140 works), and the lack of sustained aesthetic development displayed therein. When one recalls that it took Moses six years from the time she first began selling her paintings to accept her role as an artist, it becomes evident that the other three scarcely had the opportunity to grasp the implications of their changed position. Only Moses survived to enjoy a career that, spanning more than two decades, is comparable to that of any professional painter. Not since the nineteenth century had the folk artist found a market to support his or her pursuit of painting on a full-time basis.

Grandma Moses' career was a matter of demand, attitude, and longevity. The development of a demand for her work encouraged the development of a professional attitude, which, coupled with her longevity, permitted the artist to develop her style. Her background and the sources of that style made her no different from most of her colleagues. Moses was fortunate, though, in being granted more time than they and the talent to take advantage of it.

29. Lithograph used as a source by Morris Hirshfield. Photograph courtesy Sidney Janis.

Anna Mary Robertson Moses was a folk artist by birth, so to speak. Because she was rooted in the nineteenth century, her art was born of impulses that predate the promotion of "primitivism" by the elite. Throughout her career, she remained true to the tenets of nonacademic art: she did not succumb to any established style; she freely invented her own style. The availability of a professional market for her work was not so much crucial in and of itself as it was in providing an unflagging impetus for an artist who, like other amateurs, would otherwise only have painted sporadically. It takes time for any artist to hone his or her expressive skills. No oeuvre of genius is created

instantaneously. Artistic accomplishment is not the result, necessarily, of long years of formal training, but it is the result of long years of practice. With training or without, only the talented produce works of lasting merit. The masterpieces of academic art are united with those of nonacademic art in that both must transcend the achievements of their predecessors. It is not a secret revealed to the modernists alone that no great art is purely derivative. There is a level on which the nonacademic and the academic meet, where the only criterion is quality.

The struggle to liberate art from the confines of rigid aesthetic rules that motivated the pioneer modernists has often been forgotten as the success of their efforts becomes a recorded fact. Some aspects of the movement have become doctrinaire; others, relegated to the past, no longer seem vital. The alliance between folk artists and the avant-garde has been broken. The significance of a nonacademic art seems lost now that the avant-garde has become ensconced in the academies. Theoretical prescriptions governing style and form have replaced the less restrictive idealism of the early avant-garde. Sideline debates—realism versus abstraction, the elite versus the masses—have clouded the once all-important issue of artistic freedom.

With the advent of Grandma Moses, many of the problems facing nonacademic art in America came to a head. Her popular appeal, the accessible realism of her work, represented the very factors that were driving folk art away from the avant-garde. Given the general confusion surrounding folk art in America, it was easy to cast Moses into a sort of no-man's land, to deny her her folk heritage and make her the scapegoat for all those aspects of the folk tradition that disturbed progressive American art historians. Those with an elitist bias did not care to acknowledge that all folk art has populist roots. Their interest centered on older folk art, which had gone out of general fashion. They favored twentieth-century folk expression only because of its fleeting ties to the avant-garde, rather than as a valuable contribution in and of itself, and dismissed it when the ties were severed.

There was a time, theorists such as Wassily Kandinsky thought, when it should have been possible for all artists to become nonacademics: basically self-taught, independent. In those days, the example of the folk artist provided an object lesson—something to strive for. Folk art still provides such a lesson for those who are willing to learn. In its essence, nothing about it has changed. Art historical patterns come and go. The quality of the work must speak for itself.

30. **Hoosick Falls, New York, in Winter.** 1944. 20″ x 24″. The Phillips Collection, Washington, D.C. (K. 425).

CHAPTER THREE

THE DEVELOPMENT OF STYLE

Early Influences

It is almost impossible to probe the deepest origins of artistic achievement—to answer the question, "What makes a person an artist?" Anna Mary Robertson Moses lived a life that was constantly tinged by the aesthetic, whether it be found in the lush flourishing of a dogwood tree in spring or the gray-white smoke of a train against the blue hills of Virginia's Shenandoah Valley. She saw nature as a farmer sees it, and she saw it as an artist. In the end, the two points of view turned out to be very similar.

An artist's unbridled response to visual stimuli is the source of his inspiration, but the adaptation of an existing pictorial tradition is required to give form to the vision. Moses had no art background as such. She had probably never been to a museum before her own paintings were hung in one. Her tradition was the popular tradition of American landscape art, which she had come to know as a girl.

Undoubtedly, the artist never forgot her father's early encouragement. He himself was an amateur painter of some ambition (Plate 31). It is even possible that he read Rufus Porter's published treatises on landscape painting, or that he saw some of the murals Porter painted in buildings along the nearby Connecticut River Valley. In any case, Anna Mary always remembered vividly how, one winter, recovering from pneumonia, her father decided to decorate the walls of their house with scenes of the neighboring countryside. "That was a lasting wallpaper," she noted with approval.[113]

It is understandable that Moses' earliest surviving

31. Russell King Robertson. **Landscape.** Before 1900. Oil on canvas. 15½″ x 18″. The Bennington Museum, Bennington, Vermont. The full extent of Anna Mary's father's artistic endeavors cannot be determined, but in addition to his murals he is known to have completed several small canvases such as this.

efforts all evidence compositional and coloristic similarities to nineteenth-century landscape. A fireboard painted in 1918 (Plate 33) invites comparison with Porter's work (Plate 32): a unifying body of water is surrounded by foliage loosely daubed in simple earth tones. The bright hues and broad composition characteristic of Moses' mature style are completely lacking.

32. Rufus Porter. **Mural in the Joshua Eaton House, Bradford, New Hampshire.** Circa 1824. Courtesy Jean Lipman. Wall decorations such as this typify the utilitarian crafts aspect of nineteenth-century American folk art. Moses' fireboard (Plate 33) stems from the same tradition.

33. **Fireboard.** 1918. Housepaint on paper. 32¼″ x 38¾″. (K. 1). Moses, a fanatical wallpaperer, redid the house every few years. This fireboard, her earliest surviving painting, was only discovered in 1948, for it had been papered over several times.

34. George Henry Durrie (after). **Winter Morning—Feeding the Chickens.** 1863. Lithograph. Published by Currier and Ives, New York. The Harry T. Peters Collection; Museum of the City of New York.

Currier and Ives

Moses was, like many nineteenth-century folk artists, profoundly influenced by lithographic reproductions. These prints, undoubtedly the first "artistic" images the painter saw, preserved memories dear to her heart: the routine activities of country life past and present. She was especially attracted to the New England farm scenes published by Currier and Ives after paintings by George Henry Durrie. Durrie was probably the first American artist to concentrate on the native scene in winter, a subject that had, surprisingly,

been relatively ignored by the Hudson River School.[114] In works like *Winter Morning—Feeding the Chickens* (Plate 34), he presented a cozy image of rural homesteads such as Moses remembered from her childhood. In her rendition of "Winter Morning," titled *Home in Winter* (Plate 35), she followed the Durrie composition but stylized the figures. Long after she had outgrown Durrie's formal schemes, details from Currier and Ives lithographs could be detected in her paintings.

35. **Home in Winter.** Circa 1938. 6″ x 16″. (K. 38).

36. **Home in Winter** (detail).

37. **Home Among the Snowhills.**
1942. 8″ x 10″. Formerly
collection Louis J. Caldor. (K. 135).
Even when Moses copied
another composition (Plate 38),
she added her own stylistic
interpretations.

38. Chromolithographic
reproduction, possibly
taken from a greeting
card. 3⅝″ x 4⅞″.

39. Color photo-offset reproduction with Moses' pencil outlining, possibly taken from a greeting card. 4" x 2½".

40. **Night is Coming.** 1942. 8" x 10". (K. 192).

41. **Night is Coming** (detail).

Popular Illustration

Moses' earliest efforts were often verbatim copies of old prints or greeting cards, which she sometimes cut up and pasted right onto her canvas—inventing for herself the technique of collage. The artist always transformed copied source material by means of stylistic modifications: she abbreviated details that were more elaborate in the original; her rendering was impressionistic where the prototype had been precise. In *Home Among the Snowhills* (Plate 37), the two deer are reduced to a few simple brushstrokes, the tree has lost any suggestion of modeling in the trunk and its branches have become feathery, while the houses in the background melt into a whirl of snow. *Night is Coming* (Plate 40), an expansion of a rather small vignette (Plate 39), demonstrates how the components of the most mundane illustration could be transformed by Moses' hand; the bricks in the chimney have become tiny buttons of pigment (Plate 41), literally rather than illusionistically three-dimensional. The background landscape is expanded and broken into three distinct textural and formal components: the cloudy, soft distance; the vigorously brushed snow; and the stark, linear trees. Moses' presentation is, by comparison with the print, sparse, austere, and far more atmospheric.

42. **Shenandoah Valley, South Branch** and
Shenandoah Valley (1861, News of the Battle).
Circa 1938–40. Oil on oilcloth. 19¾″ x 14″
and 20½″ x 16¼″, respectively. Private
collection. (K. 51 and 52). Accounts vary as to
how, exactly, the artist came to cut the painting
in half. Apparently, she had promised Louis
Caldor one more picture than she was able to
deliver and therefore devised this clever
solution.

43. **Shenandoah Valley
(1861, News of the Battle)**
(detail). In her early
work, Moses often used
sticks and even matches
to paint small details,
which as a result look
somewhat crude.

44. Four-color magazine illustration with Moses' pencil outlining. Approximately 10″ x 7″. The artist conceived an original composition (Plate 42) by cutting up a clipping and rearranging its component parts. She used a sewing needle to pin the images together.

45. **Autumn in the Berkshires.** Before 1927. Housepaint on threshing-machine canvas. 8″x 14¼″. Formerly collection Louis J. Caldor. (K. 8).

46. **Autumn in the Berkshires.** "Worsted" embroidery. 9″ x 21¾″. Formerly collection Louis J. Caldor. (K. 1W).

Technique

Moses was a "primitive" twice over: first, because she had never received instruction in the technique of painting, and second, because she did not have access to professional equipment. In the beginning, she recalled, "Sometimes I had to use a match [to render fine details]."[115] One guesses that this may have been the method used to portray the barn in *Home in Winter* (Plate 36) or the structure of the house (Plate 72) in *On the Road to Greenwich.* For the tiny eyes and mouths of her figures, she needed a straight pin.

Later, of course, her thoughtful patrons saw to it that she had proper tools. And, with practice, she was able to overcome her lack of formal art training by developing highly effective methods of her own. Still, Grandma's typically self-effacing explanation for the improving quality of her work—that it was "owing to better brushes and paint"[116]—contained an element of truth.

For whatever reason, Moses was initially able to achieve greater precision with yarn than with paint. *Autumn in the Berkshires* (Plate 45), that very early effort daubed in house-paint on a scrap of threshing-machine canvas, is crude in relation to her embroidered version (Plate 46). Comparison of painted and stitched renditions of similar subjects (Plates 47 and 48) shows that the artist tried to duplicate the effects

of needlework in paint. She was inclined to apply pigment the same way she applied yarn: in broad, smooth swaths, or short, stitchlike dabs (Plates 49 and 50). Experience with embroidery taught her to isolate blocks of color, to break forms into their component hues. It is perhaps from this that the impressionistic aspects of her style stem.

The constraints of working with yarn actually seem to have conditioned the artist's visual perceptions. Because embroidery does not allow the blending of colors or the modeling of form, she had to invent other solutions to these problems. She learned to build tonalities by layering or interspersing different hues. Details, such as figures, that did not lend themselves to such interpretations were simply rendered as flat shapes.

Compositionally, too, one may see a relationship between Moses' paintings and her needlework. There is a sense that all her landscapes are sewn together, with details inset like decorative appliqués. An overriding concern with patterning gives some of her pictures a quiltlike quality, which is, on occasion, accentuated by a grid-structure of multicolored fields. Certainly, if Moses' iconographic roots lay in nineteenth-century lithography, her stylistic roots may be found in embroidery.

47. **House and Flower Garden.** Circa 1931. "Worsted" embroidery. 11″ x 14″. Collection Mr. and Mrs. George O. Cook. (K. 26W).

48. **By the Sea.** 1942. 11½″ x 15¾″. (K. 178). Note how the flowers in this painting seem "sewn" into place.

49. **The Covered Bridge, 1818.** 1939 or earlier. "Worsted" embroidery. Formerly collection Louis J. Caldor. 7½" x 9½". (K. 13W).

50. **The Old Automobile** (detail). The contrast between flat expanses of paint and "embroidered" details such as the bushes and fence suggests an approach similar to that found in the artist's needlework pictures.

51. **The Old Automobile.** 1944. 18¾″ x 21½″. Private collection. (K. 442). Moses became well known for "memory pictures" like this one depicting the introduction of the automobile to rural America. The concept would prove popular with later folk painters of the twentieth century.

52. **Checkered House.** 1955. 18" x 24". (K. 1165). The "Old Checkered House" was an inn in the old town of Cambridge, not far from the Moses homestead. Its distinctive red and white checkerboard front and its historical connection with the Revolutionary War made it a famous landmark even after its destruction by fire in 1907.

A Hobby Becomes an Art

Copying greeting cards and doing "fancy work" were activities well within the limits of nineteenth-century home-making. Today, a few otherwise undistinguished nine-teenth-century women are remembered because they transcended this framework to create works that qualify as art.[117] Grandma Moses, in the twentieth century, manifested a similar resourcefulness in her embroideries and paintings. The stylistic ingenuity of even her more derivative work placed it beyond the ordinary. Like many before her, however, she also turned to her immediate surroundings for inspiration. The urge to record her memories, her own farm, and local legends such as the *Checkered House* (Plates 52 and 53) and *The Old Oaken Bucket* (Plates 54 and 57), soon led her away from straight copying. Thus the desire to have something pretty around the house sparked a talent for conceiving original works of art.

Increasing technical abilities accompanied the expansion of the artist's creative resources. The economic ramifications of her transition from hobbyist to artist removed the con-straints of amateurism that had often hindered her female predecessors. Furthermore, the development of a market for her work forced her to come to terms, aesthetically, with the various demands that were put upon her. Some requests challenged her ingenuity; others entailed inappropriate solu-

53. **Checkered House.** 1943. Oil on canvas. 36″ x 45″. IBM Corporation, Armonk, New York. (K. 317).

tions. She learned to cope with the first sort and ignore the second. Most important, she learned to tell the difference.

"When I first commenced to paint with oil," Moses explained, "I thought every painting would be my last one, so I was not so interested. Then the requests commenced to come for this one and that one. 'Paint me one just like that one!'"[118] Grandma's earliest customers, who came or wrote to Eagle Bridge for her pictures, were very explicit about their desires. "Will you paint me...an 'OLD OAKEN BUCKET' size: width—26¾ inches, height—21½ inches, rather like the one you did recently for Mrs. Story....Do you remember it? It shapes up to a high hill in the center."[119] The writer of this letter even included a small sketch to prod Grandma's memory. Moses, for her part, perhaps recalling Caldor's warning against copying other works of art, was

leery of copying herself. Sidney Janis tried to dispel her worries: "To do another VERSION of a painting of YOUR OWN has been done by all great artists of the past and present. Remember you are *not copying*. It is another version—one with *more* and *clearer details*."[120] Moses apparently came to accept this rationale, for a number of themes recur in her oeuvre, among them, not just the "Old Oaken Bucket" and the "Checkered House," but "Sugaring Off," "Catching the Thanksgiving Turkey," and "Out for Christmas Trees." Nonetheless, she never repeated a single composition exactly. When one considers that Edward Hicks produced sixty-odd variations of the *Peaceable Kingdom*, or that many academic artists have duplicated especially popular canvases, Moses' inventiveness can be appreciated in context.

54. The Old Oaken Bucket. 1946. 20″ x 24½″. Formerly collection Helen Hayes. (K. 616). The artist explained her renditions of the "Old Oaken Bucket" theme by citing a local legend about the author of the lyrics to the popular song. However, it should be mentioned that while the Moses composition is entirely original, the subject was a common one in nineteenth-century America and appears in a Currier and Ives lithograph (Plate 23) as well as in folk paintings of the time (Plate 24).

55. The Old Oaken Bucket (detail). The mill, a standard feature of the "Bucket" story, was a highly imaginative stylization of a rather mundane illustration (Plate 56).

56. *Far right:* Color photo-offset reproduction with Moses' pencil outlining. 6″ x 3¾″.

57. **The Old Oaken Bucket, the Last.** 1946. 36″ x 48″. Oil on canvas. Collection Mr. and Mrs. Garson Kanin. (K. 576). This is not the artist's last version, though one may surmise that the title is a personal comment on a frequently requested subject.

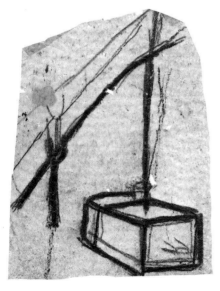

58. **The Old Well.** Pencil on thin paper. Approximately 3″ x 2½″. Moses probably used this simple outline sketch as the prototype for the wells in all her "Bucket" paintings.

59. **White Christmas.** 1954. 23¾″ x 19¾″. Collection Mr. and Mrs. Irving Berlin. (K. 1162).

Friendly Suggestions

Along with the orders came advice of all kinds: "finish up the details more," "paint simpler," "don't paint too thin," "hurry up," "take your time." Moses received the various comments politely (sometimes by "forgetting" to acknowledge them), but she was not about to let anyone push her around. In response to an inquiry concerning religious subjects, she at first replied, "I might try some, thank you for the suggestion."[121] Several months later she wrote the same customer, "Someone has asked me to paint Biblical pictures, and I say *no*, I'll not paint something that we know nothing about, might just as well paint something that will happen a thousand years hence."[122] Nor did she respond favorably to Kallir's idea that her style would be well-suited to children's book illustrations: "Have been trying to paint for the child's book, but did not like them so painted them over. But will keep on trying. But I don't take much stock in books."[123] At another point, it was suggested that she depart from her usual horizontal landscape format so that her pictures could be more easily reproduced on magazine covers. The relatively small number of verticals in her oeuvre attests to the lack of enthusiasm with which she greeted this proposal. Moses was equally adamant about continuing to strew glitter on her snow scenes to make them sparkle, something which, she was cautioned, no respectable artist should do. She also refused to alter her brightly colored skies, which some found too reminiscent of gaudy chromos: "I love pink, and the pink skies are beautiful," she insisted. "Even as a child, the redder I got my skies with my father's old paint, the prettier they were."[124]

Though Moses' patrons sometimes offered conflicting suggestions, on one thing they were all agreed: she should paint larger. "You have done more than enough small pictures," Caldor told her early on, and sent her bigger canvas boards to work on. Several years later, Kallir voiced a similar request. "Mr. Kallir, Dear Sir," she replied with typical astuteness, "You asked for larger canvases. You can have them. But they will cost more."[125] It was Ala Story who got Moses to paint her largest pieces by providing her with specially prepared canvases in sizes up to thirty-six by

60. Grandma Moses at her "tip-up" table (K. 2). 1948. Photograph by Otto Kallir. The table, which dated from the eighteenth century, had been handed down to her by an aunt several years after the artist returned to New York with her family. Moses decorated it with painted landscape scenes and collage. The tip-up top was designed so that the piece, in its original incarnation as a dining table, could be easily stored; but when Moses used it as a painting surface she kept the top in its horizontal position.

forty-eight inches (Plate 94). "I am quite excited to get a big canvas," Story wrote the artist. "There is no need that you paint the houses, horses, etc., much bigger—just a little—but there will be a wider landscape and I think you may find it fun."[126] Moses did not find it altogether "fun," as the canvases were too big to fit on the "tip-up" table at which she usually painted (Plate 60). Instead, they were laid flat on her bed, which she had to circumnavigate to reach all sides of the painting. In later years, the strain of this exercise became too much for her, and she had to forego extremely large work.

Moses was not entirely pleased with her biggest paintings, calling them "really too large to be pretty."[127] Her aesthetic judgment was still conditioned by smaller-format art reproductions. Nonetheless, the suggestions she received from her patrons were crucial in encouraging her to emerge from the confines of her source material. By expanding her proportions, she was able, quite literally, to expand her horizons.

61. Moses working on the painting **Williamstown in Winter** (K. 759). 1948. Photograph by Otto Kallir.

62. **The Dearest Spot on Earth.** 1940. 7¾″ x 9¾″. Private collection. (K. 18). Though the print below (Plate 63) has been reinterpreted in Moses' inimitable style, she elected to make few compositional changes.

Expanding Horizons

From the start, the artist had not been satisfied with the conventional approach to landscape presented in lithographs and magazine illustrations. Images like Durrie's, with relatively low horizon lines, tended to incorporate nature primarily as a backdrop for architectural and genre elements (Plate 63). "Pure" landscapes (Plate 65), on the other hand, lacked the anecdotal facets Moses cherished. She was interested in portraying foreground and distance simultaneously. She was attracted by the immediacy of the close-up, but she also desired a panorama. It occurred to her that she could achieve greater range by combining two or more copied images in one painting. In so doing, she merged two elements that artists before her were inclined to treat separately (Plate 64).

63. Color photo-offset reproduction with Moses' pencil outlining. 6″ x 8″.

64. **Down in the Valley.** 1945. 10″ x 12″. Private collection. (K. 512). Two conventional landscape views (Plates 63 and 65) are merged in an unconventional manner.

65. Chromolithographic reproduction with Moses' pencil outlining. 5⅜″ x 7¼″.

66. **Harpers Ferry.** 1953. 12″ x 18″. Formerly collection Louis J. Caldor. (K. 1095).

In Currier and Ives's view of Harper's Ferry (Plate 67), a broad vista is revealed from the vantage point of a small plateau, a common academic formal device. Moses, in her rendering of a similar scene (Plate 66), forces the entire village into the foreground. She wants to enjoy the houses, the trees, the activities of the local folk, *and* she wants the larger landscape too. Conversely, in *The First Skating* (Plate 68), she is not satisfied with Currier and Ives's cluttered crowd scene (Plate 69). Careful comparison of the two images reveals that Moses culled those skaters she found interesting and then incorporated them in a far deeper and more varied panorama.

67. **View of Harper's Ferry, Va. (From the Potomac Side).**
Lithograph. Published by Currier and Ives, New York. The Harry T. Peters Collection; Museum of the City of New York.

68. **The First Skating.** 1945. 17¾"
x 23". Private collection.
(K. 486).

69. **Central Park, Winter—
The Skating Pond.** 1862.
Lithograph. Published by
Currier and Ives, New
York. The Harry T. Peters
Collection; Museum of the
City of New York.

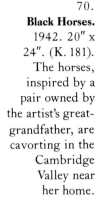

70.
Black Horses.
1942. 20″ x 24″. (K. 181). The horses, inspired by a pair owned by the artist's great-grandfather, are cavorting in the Cambridge Valley near her home.

Moses had spent most of her life surrounded by hills and valleys, so it was natural for her to approach nature from an elevated perspective. Even among her earliest endeavors there were some that presented a "bird's-eye view" of the local environment. One of these, *On the Road to Greenwich* (Plate 73), adopts this approach without violating convention: the artist does not allow her fascination with the patterning of fields and foliage free reign, nor does she add anecdotal elements. Remarkable in its range of colors—from the brittle yellow of late-summer fields to the pale blue of distant hills—this painting was one of those that convinced Otto Kallir to give the artist her first show.

By 1942 Moses had begun to freely interweave landscape and genre elements. *Black Horses* (Plate 70) is actually less academic than some of her earlier work; she has abandoned aerial perspective for a more schematized approach to space. In fact, the painting was so marked in its stylistic independence that Kallir considered it a turning point in his evaluation of the artist. The view was more extensive than previously, the patchwork of multicolored fields treated more abstractly, the whole more eloquently composed. Suddenly, the artist was responding to shapes and colors as autonomous entities, freeing them from a merely illusionistic function. The pastel blocks of color that form the fields (Plate 71), the tiny houses, and the meticulously daubed trees and hedgerows were knit together into an imaginative construct that was entirely of the artist's making. She had finally broken free of her copied sources; from now on, they would do her bidding, not she theirs.

71. **Black Horses** (detail). The abstract treatment of the houses and fields produces an integrated composition.

72. **On the Road to Greenwich** (detail). In her earliest works, the artist strove more for three-dimensional verisimilitude.

73. **On the Road to Greenwich.** 1940 or earlier. 14″ x 22″. Formerly collection Louis J. Caldor. (K. 26). Because of its primitive incorporation of aerial perspective, this depiction of the Cambridge Valley is actually more academic than the artist's later version (Plate 70). Paintings with specific titles such as this usually portray real places in the New York or Virginia communities where she lived.

74. Mt. Nebo in Winter (detail). Variations in texture are used to distinguish the white building from its snowy surroundings.

75. **Mt. Nebo in Winter** (detail).

76. **Mt. Nebo in Winter.** 1943. 20½″ x 26½″. Private collection. (K. 275). "Mt. Nebo," the Biblical mountain where Moses disappeared, was the family nickname for their last farm in Virginia and later for the farm they bought in Eagle Bridge, New York. This painting depicts the Eagle Bridge homestead, which is recognizable in many of the artist's paintings. The undulating hills and valleys of the surrounding countryside inspired her approach to landscape composition.

child Hood Home. amma Mary RobertSon. Moses.

77. **The Childhood Home of Anna Mary Robertson Moses.** 1942. 14″ x 28″. Formerly collection Louis J. Caldor. (K. 160). The latitude of a "memory" subject such as this allowed the artist's imagination free reign. Her feeling for abstract pattern (perhaps derived from her needlework background) and her appreciation of broad vistas were complementary components of the "Grandma Moses style."

The Grandma Moses Style

The inspiration that enabled Moses to crystallize her method came to her quite suddenly. "In the yard one day," she related, "there was a new car with those big, shiny hubcaps. I happened to glance down and see in one of them a perfect little picture. It was distorted, of course, by the round cap, but there were the figures of the people, the green trees, the reflection of the house—everything: a perfect little picture, far better than the ones I had been copying. Well, . . . I went back and found a window, on the porch, that had the same perfect picture reflected in it. The perspective, the colors. By moving a little this way or that, I could frame the view just the way I wanted it. There it was."[128]

Often asked for help by aspiring amateurs, Grandma later instructed them to follow this procedure. However, the revelation of the reflected landscape was for her important chiefly as a catalyst. She did not employ the device every time she organized a composition. Moses painted indoors, mainly from memory and an intuitive design sense. Though she judged it impractical to paint *au plein air,* she did occasionally make on-the-spot sketches. She also asked family members to photograph various local vistas for her, so that she could pinpoint specific details. She almost never copied an entire landscape from a photograph or print. She studied these sources to learn how hills undulate and blend with each other and with clusters of fields and trees, the way roads curve and narrow into the distance. Then she went upstairs to her bedroom studio and painted "mostly emanation" as she called it.[129]

Moses was evolving a standard procedure for making paintings. Like many artists, she worked on several at a time, switching back and forth according to mood and inspiration. She attributed this habit to "Scotch thrift," as it allowed her to make the fullest use of the colors she had prepared. "Saves lots of paint to work this way," she explained. "Don't all dry up on you."[130] When she was done, she preferred to give her work time to "settle." "I like to finish up a painting and then study it for a week or ten days," she wrote. "Most always see then where one can improve

it."[131] Asked whether she had any particular color theories, she replied, "I haven't any at all, but there's no gettin' away from it, certain colors fascinate me. Take this bluish green edgin' my apron. I could almost eat that color, I like it so well."[132] She was just as vague about her preference for various types of subjects: "Some appeal to me, others do not, and therefore I cannot do them justice."[133]

Moses was not long on complex aesthetic explanations, but it was clear that she knew what she wanted. She spoke about painting with a deep, intuitive knowledge. "As Grandma Moses talked of the technique of painting," recalled a reporter for *The New York Herald Tribune*, "a curious look came over her face, and suddenly she was no longer a quaint figure nor [*sic*] a curiosity. For the look was the intense vision of the working artist, which has nothing to do with withered hands or age. In that swift glimpse the visitor could see that Grandma Moses, untaught, uneducated, with very little understanding of her own gifts, is a true artist."[134]

Grandma's growing artistic ability was favorably noted in the reviews of her two 1944 exhibitions at the Galerie St. Etienne. "With each succeeding show," wrote one critic, "the artist continues to be a better painter, more assured in her technical resources, more skilled in composition, less concerned with her quaintness as a value in her work."[135] "Her figure drawing is primitive and her perspective knows no known rules," noted another, "but she can paint trees, for example, with a rather startling technique—part neo-impressionism, part pointillism, mostly Grandma Moses. Her brush technique . . . is far better than she has been given credit for."[136]

Without altogether realizing it, Moses was educating herself. She was accumulating bits of knowledge and adapting them to her own ends. She was learning to be an artist. The old prints and newer ones that she cut out of magazines, her embroidery techniques coupled with practical experience, a more conscious awareness of the local landscape—all were gradually incorporated in a single, original style.

79. **Wind Storm.** 1956. 16″ x 24″. Private collection. (K. 1250).

80. Halftone newspaper illustration with Moses' pencil outlining. 3⅞″ x 10½″. Moses incorporated both the woman and the threshing machine as discrete elements in her painting **Wind Storm** (Plate 79).

CHAPTER FOUR

HOW DID SHE PAINT?

Transcending Her Sources

As Grandma Moses learned to formulate her own compositions, the role played by clippings from magazines and greeting cards changed. Though she no longer copied them outright, she continued to collect them. For an artist who had never been taught to draw the human body from a live model, or to render buildings three-dimensionally, these images remained instructive. While she perceived nature sensuously, she perceived figures and objects formally. Clippings thus became catalysts that suggested approaches to both form and subject matter. Moses' vision was able to distill from the most mundane sources essences of abstract design and human meaning that far transcended their humble origins. She was, in short, able to extract the element of universal potency that gives popular illustration its appeal by replacing its original stylistic and referential context with her own.

Although it is known that nonacademic artists from Hicks to Hirshfield relied on printed images, little evidence survives to show how this material was used by them. The instructional essays of Rufus Porter suggest that the method was far more deliberate and refined than these so-called "primitives" are usually given credit for. Porter provided his readers with illustrations of stock landscape forms and encouraged them to create files of "outline drawings...of various kinds, sizes and positions on paper; the back sides of these papers are to be brushed over with dry venetian red;

then by placing one of the papers against the wall, and tracing the outlines...a copy thereof is transferred to the wall ready for coloring."[137]

Such an assortment of models in varying sizes facilitated a short-cut approach to perspective. "Every object must be painted larger or smaller according to the distance at which it is represented," Porter instructed. "By these means, the view will apparently recede from the eye, and will have a very striking effect."[138] One may imagine that Moses, employing a similar method, arranged her clippings on the canvas to test compositions. "I paint from the top down," she told one interviewer. "As you get lower down on the picture, things get bigger, you know," she added confidentially.[139]

Guided by this general principle, and by the larger structure provided by her observations of the landscape, Moses interpolated elements derived from her clippings. These prints no longer served as compositional sources. Often, in fact, as in *Wind Storm* (Plates 79 and 80), she deliberately broke up existing configurations. She had no qualms about taking a winter scene—such as the clipping (Plate 84) used for *A Beautiful World* (Plate 83)—and giving it a summer context, or vice versa. If a clipping did not exactly fit, she felt free to alter it. Usually the clippings retain pencil lines indicating how she intended to simplify or change the basic shapes.

81. **Wind Storm** (detail, Plate 79). While they remain entirely recognizable, Moses' vignettes are more symbolic than realistic.

82. **A Beautiful World** (detail). Lack of specific detailing gives these dancing figures an allegorical presence; they represent not actual people but rather an emotional response to nature.

83. **A Beautiful World.** 1948. 20″ x 24″. Private collection. (K. 787). The artist often painted idealized farm scenes that, though based on observed phenomena, did not relate to any particular real-life location.

84. Chromolithographic reproduction with Moses' pencil outlining. 5⅝″ x 8¼″. Moses extracted the formal configurations of the house and tree (Plates 85 and 86) from this clipping, but did not use it as a compositional guide.

85. **A Beautiful World**
(detail, Plate 83).

86.
**A Beautiful
World** (detail,
Plate 83).

87. **Joy Ride** (detail). The beckoning figure in the doorway is a common motif in Moses' work.

Recurring Motifs

In addition to formal details, printed images provided the artist with visual correlatives for remembered experiences. Each small vignette sparked a recollection of some aspect of rural life. She thus sought out clippings that would capture the full variety of that life, continually collecting more to supplement the existing group and replace those that wore out. Specific clippings were used to conceive isolated elements, and for this purpose Moses accumulated a wide selection of recurring motifs (men with plows, for example) that gave her the flexibility she needed (Plates 90, 92, and 96). A single painting was composed of a great many individual images: barns, houses, people, and animals, all assembled according to schematic perspective and spontaneous design. Because the artist reused the clippings, it is not surprising that similar figures resurface in different paintings. She was fond of certain general pictorial conventions, possibly derived from nineteenth-century lithographs, such as the woman in the doorway (Plate 87) who may be found in *Joy Ride* (Plate 88) and countless other works. For her "theme" paintings, such as *Catching the Thanksgiving Turkey* or *Checkered House*, she had specialized clippings that were employed only for these subjects. Every image was provided with a purpose to suit her needs. Men loading barrels (Plate 101) might be packing up to leave in *Moving Day on the Farm* (Plates 98 and 102) or delivering the evening's refreshment in *Halloween* (Plate 104). Each time she interpreted and combined the elements anew.

88. **Joy Ride.** 1953. 18″ x 24″. (K. 1079).

89. **In Harvest Time.** 1945. 18″ x 28½″. Private collection. (K. 537).

90. Halftone newspaper illustration with Moses' pencil outlining. 3½″ x 5¾″.

91. **In Harvest Time** (detail).

92. Halftone magazine illustration with Moses' pencil outlining. Approximately 3⅜" x 4¼". Clippings such as this were used as sources for various aspects of farm scenery and activities.

93. **In Harvest Time** (detail).

94. **Grandma Moses Going to Big City.** 1946. Oil on canvas. 36″ x 48″. Private collection. (K. 577). This canvas, one of the artist's largest, incorporates a number of already familiar elements, including the Eagle Bridge farm.

95. **Grandma Moses Going to Big City** (detail). The formal simplicity of Moses' style allowed her to combine a multitude of anecdotal details without an overwhelming sense of busyness.

96. Two-color line illustration with Moses' pencil outlining, taken from a 1942 issue of *The Watchtower*. 3½″ x 3¼″.

97. **Grandma Moses Going to Big City** (detail).

98. **Moving Day on the Farm** (detail). Moses' appreciation of the infinite variety of farm equipment and animals prevented the repetition of these images from becoming tedious.

99. **Moving Day on the Farm** (detail).

100. **Moving Day on the Farm.** 1951. 17″ x 22″. Galerie St. Etienne, New York. (K. 965).

101. Four-color magazine illustration with Moses'
pencil outlining. Approximately 3½″ x 6″. Some
clippings, like this one, served a number of purposes,
because they could be adapted to suit the subject at hand.

102. **Moving Day on the Farm** (detail, Plate 100). The context of the painting provides the vignette with its specific meaning,
which here clearly relates to the moving process.

103. **Halloween** (detail). The ethereal quality of this "ghost" house contrasts with the merriment in the foreground of the painting, where the men from the clipping (Plate 101) appear with a load of cider.

104. **Halloween.** 1955. 18″ x 24″. (K. 1188).

105. **Missouri.** 1943. 20″ x 23¾″. Galerie St. Etienne, New York. (K. 224). This landscape, which looks suspiciously like upstate New York, was inspired by a poem, "Where the Muddy Missouri Rolls."

106. **Hoosick Valley.** 1942. 15¼″ x 20½″. Galerie St. Etienne, New York. (K. 174). This and the following two plates depict the view from the window of the artist's bedroom studio.

Color

As Moses learned to work with the clippings, which formed the basis for her anecdotal details, she also studied the hues and forms of nature, which provided the unifying context for her paintings. Her daughter-in-law Dorothy often observed her looking out the window to analyze "the various shades of green and the bark colors."[140] "Often I get at a loss to know just which shade of green," the artist explained. "There are a hundred trees that have each three or four shades of green in them. I look at a tree and I see the limbs, and then the next part of a tree is a dark, dark, black-green, then I have got to make a little lighter green, and so on. And then on the outside, it'll either be a yellow green, or whitish green, that's the way the trees are shaded."[141] Moses was not willing to accept the word of those who proposed a more conventional approach to the landscape if it contradicted her experience: "And the snow—they tell me I should shade it more, or use more blue, but I have looked at the snow and looked at the snow, and I can see no blue, sometimes there is a little shadow of a tree, but that would be gray, instead of blue, as I see it."[142]

107. **Hoosick Valley (from the Window)** (detail). Texture and abstraction—two aspects of the artist's style that derive from needlework—are used to define the distant townscape and the trompe-l'oeil curtain.

Texture

Moses knew that there were many hues in the summer landscape, and if she could see no blue in snow, she could, with remarkable ingenuity, solve the complex problem of painting a white house on a white field (Plate 74) or a stack of golden hay in a golden meadow (Plate 91). She used brushstrokes to isolate these elements by giving them three-dimensional solidity. Color was applied like strands of yarn in an embroidery—one separate stroke upon another. She thus created a complex network of pigment composed of multiple layers of varying density. Usually working with pure, rather than blended tones (very often she squeezed the paint directly from the tube onto her brush), Moses established a series of textural gradations, from flat expanses and isolated blocks of color to more intricate, multihued configurations. This overall structure facilitated the integration of the anecdotal components by easing the transitions between figure and landscape.

108. **Hoosick Valley (from the Window).** 1946. 19½″ x 22″. Private collection. (K. 611).

109.
**Covered Bridge
with Carriage.**
1946. 27½″ x
21½″. The
Shelburne
Museum,
Shelburne,
Vermont.
(K. 645).

"SHADY VALLEY   R. W. Woicot

110. Two line illustrations
attached with a straight
pin. 4⅞" x 5⅞".

111. **Horse and Buggy.**
Pencil on thin paper. 2¼" x 4".

112. Halftone newspaper
illustration with Moses' pencil
outlining. Approximately
2¼" x 3⅝".

Composition

Moses generally composed her painting by drawing directly on the Masonite board that was her preferred support (Plate 61). She had little need for preliminary drawings, using them chiefly as substitutes for clippings that could not be cut out and saved. If, for example, she were attracted to an illustration in a book, which she would not want to destroy, she copied it neatly on a sheet of paper. Occasionally, as in *Covered Bridge with Carriage* (Plate 109), she made a drawing (Plate 111) in order to reverse a printed image (Plate 112). Though she rarely found it desirable to block out a complete compositional sketch on paper, she did make drawings of subordinate figural groupings. She is also known to have tried out arrangements in advance by pinning two or more clippings together—a strange mixture of the seamstress's and painter's arts (Plate 110). If, while painting, she saw that some configurations did not work as she had planned them, she felt free to make changes. Sometimes she thought it necessary, for balance, to add or remove elements. She made such corrections with turpentine and a rag if the paint were still wet or, if not, by scraping with a palette knife.[143]

**113. Catching the
Thanksgiving Turkey**
(detail). The blue pencil
lines of the artist's
underlying compositional
sketch are clearly visible.

The artist's approach to composition was additive. She
expanded upon her source material by visually pulling it
apart and fusing new elements onto it. A relatively small
black and white vignette (Plate 116) seems to have served as
the nucleus for her many "Catching the Thanksgiving Turkey" scenes. In the version owned by the Metropolitan
Museum of Art (Plate 118), the barn and grindstone in the
original are placed at a greater distance from each other and
supplemented by a whole new "cast of characters," as well as
by a more complex background landscape. In a slightly
earlier rendition (Plate 114), Moses used some of the figures
from the clipping, but neither the barn nor the grindstone.
She supplemented these with an appropriate array of people,
birds, and buildings of both thematic and formal relevance.
A rare drawing (Plate 115) shows how deliberately these
elements were arranged. The sketch corresponds fairly
closely to the painting, but there are modifications in the
finished version; the child standing next to the woman has
been eliminated, as has the brace of prancing ponies or dogs
to the right. A large male turkey has been replaced by a pair
of females, and this flock of birds has been turned around
to focus attention directly on the central activity of the piece.

114. **Catching the Thanksgiving Turkey.** 1943. 20″ x 24″. Private Collection. (K. 231). An existing popular pictorial tradition is here amplified by the artist's personal observations.

115. Study for **Catching the Thanksgiving Turkey** (Plate 114). Pencil on verso of sheet of wallpaper. Approximately 5½″ x 23½″. Various figural groupings taken from clippings (Plates 116 and 117) are reduced to their barest outlines and rearranged in an original composition.

116. Halftone magazine illustration with Moses' pencil outlining. 4⅛″ x 7⅛″.

117. Two-color magazine illustration with Moses' pencil outlining. 1½″ x 3″.

118.
Thanksgiving Turkey. 1943. 15⅛″ x 19⅛″. The Metropolitan Museum of Art, New York; Bequest of Mary Stillman Harkness, 1950. (K. 293). Though based on the same clipping (Plate 116) as the previous version (Plate 114), the composition in this painting is entirely different.

119. **December** (detail). Compositional unity as well as atmospheric effect are achieved by a harmonious blending of simple colors, which here convey the sense of an impending snowstorm.

120. **December.** 1943. 18½″ x 21¾″. Estate of Otto Kallir. (K. 287). Note the reappearance of the shepherd and flock from Plate 114, as well as a variation of the "woman-in-the-doorway" motif.

121. **Out for Christmas Trees.**
1946. 26″ x 36″. Private
collection. (K. 606). Moses,
uncomfortable painting interior
scenes, was dissatisfied with her
depictions of the Christmas
holiday until a friend suggested
she concentrate on the
preliminary activities of
tree selection.

122.
Out for Christmas Trees
(detail). Though the artist's
vignettes are well integrated
with the overall composition,
most also function as
independent entities.

123. **Horse and Sleigh.** Pencil on thin paper. 2⅜″ x 2¼″. A sketch like this one was reusable, and would be incorporated in a picture according to aesthetic and contextual considerations.

124. **Out for Christmas Trees** (detail). The abstract quality of Moses' figures may be traced to her linear approach to form (Plate 123).

125. **The Spring in Evening.** 1947. 27″ x 21″. Private collection. (K. 706).

126. **The Spring in Evening** (detail). Natural elements are built up with layers of color.

127. **The Spring in Evening** (detail). The structural simplicity of such figural groupings contrasts with the textured tonalities of the landscape.

Realism

While Moses' way of piecing together compositions was partly dictated by her sense of abstract design, the arrangements were always subordinated to the requirements of the landscape. As a substitute for academic perspective, she had recourse not just to a progressive scheme of diminishing sizes, but also to coloristic indicators of space. She was quick to note such qualities as the pale blue of distant hills or the tonal gradations of the sky. She translated phenomena observed from nature into veils of color and layers of pigment. The rich browns and greens of a fertile spring hillside (Plate 126), the shimmering weight of fresh-fallen snow (Plate 128), the orange glow on the horizon beneath threatening storm clouds (Plate 136), are described with a textural richness that gives both structure and meaning to the artist's work. Variations in the physical and tonal density of the paint create a series of transitions between the anecdotal vignettes and the more complex hues of the landscape. The vignettes are spare formal essences embedded in a network of paint: the bold silhouette of proud horses (Plate 127), the icy cascade of a waterwheel (Plate 130), and the upturned half-moon of a girl's face (Plate 137).

128. **A Frosty Day.** 1951. 18″ x 24″. Estate of Otto Kallir. (K. 985).

129. **A Frosty Day** (detail). Moses' "snow" usually has a three-dimensional presence, while her figures are flat.

130. **A Frosty Day** (detail). Note how paint density is used to mimic the tactile sensation of flowing water.

131.
The Thunderstorm
(detail).

132. **The Thunderstorm.** 1948. 20¾″ x 24¾″. Private collection. (K. 729).

133.
**The
Thunderstorm**
(detail).

134. **The Thunderstorm** (detail).

Storm Scenes

Moses' style was an amalgam of disparate entities precisely balanced—genre and landscape, the painterly and the flat, realism and abstraction—the whole held together by harmonious composition and deft brushwork. Her intertwining of figural and natural elements is perhaps most dramatically demonstrated by her storm scenes. In a painting like *The Thunderstorm* (Plate 132), the rhythmically choreographed actions of the people and animals echo the force of the wind. The trees toss wildly against an ominous sky (Plate 131), and horses bolt in a frenzy (Plate 134). The static forms of the buildings and some of the figures set off those elements that are in motion (Plate 133), thereby providing both structural unity and dramatic counterpoint. Similarly, the solid slabs of paint used for the anecdotal components may be contrasted with the impressionistic brushwork of the surrounding scenery. The artist has accurately translated the sensations of the storm into color and shape, while retaining a highly stylized view of the creatures and objects.

135. **Taking in Laundry.** 1951. 17″ x 21¾″. Private collection. (K. 967). Moses' compositions often have a narrative structure. Here, the progress of the approaching storm is described by a series of anecdotal details (Plates 136 and 137), while the women in the foreground blithely proceed with their washing.

137. **Taking in Laundry** (detail).

138. Four-color
magazine illustra-
tion with Moses'
pencil outlining.
7½" x 10¼". The
tonal gradations of
this commercial
illustration were of
no concern to
Moses, who was
more interested in
basic shapes
(Plate 139).

139. **Hoosick River,
Summer** (detail).

140. **Hoòsick River, Summer.** 1952. 18″ x 24″. Private collection. (K. 1032).

Abstraction

Whereas her landscapes were painted with an atmospheric buildup of tonal layers, Moses' figures were always rendered with a few plain jolts of pigment. The latter, often derived from clippings, were nonetheless not straight copies, but rather abstractions. As clearly revealed by her drawings, the artist perceived objects in terms of line, transferring their contours in pencil to her Masonite panel. She painted without direct reference to her source material, relying on it only occasionally for color guidelines (generally the prints were black and white) and almost never for shading. The elements were reduced to simple shapes and filled in with neat, flat strokes of paint. The result was highly abstract, as typified by the children (Plate 139) in *Hoosick River, Summer* (Plate 140) or the two running boys (Plate 143) in *Little Boy Blue* (Plate 141).

141. **Little Boy Blue.** 1947. 20½″ x 23″. Private collection. (K. 660). Moses was drawn to preexisting themes that reflected aspects of rural life.

142. **Little Boy Blue** (detail). The story of the "cows in the corn" and the boys (Plate 143) running to alert the sleeping "boy blue" has been subtly embedded in the larger landscape.

143. **Little Boy Blue** (detail).

144. **Early Springtime on the Farm.** 1945. 16″ x 25¾″. Private collection. (K. 500).

145. **Early Springtime on the Farm** (detail).

146. Two-color photo-offset reproduction with Moses' pencil outlining and glitter. 3¾″ x 3⅛″.

147. **Early Springtime on the Farm** (detail). Here Moses' stylistic alterations were so great that there is little resemblance between the painted image and the clipping (Plate 146) from which it derives.

148. **Hoosick River, Winter.** 1952. 18″ x 24″. Private collection. (K. 1031). The brittle browns and grays of this sparse landscape have a sensory immediacy that invites identification with the narrative details.

149. **Hoosick River, Winter** (detail). The painting can be "read" from left to right as a series of incidents culminating in the crack of the gun that causes the pheasants to take wing.

Stylistic Synthesis

Moses' abstract melding of shapes transcended not only the stylistic limitations of her source material, but its narrative aspect as well. If early lithography had taken the pictorial conventions of academic painting and subordinated them to popular content, Moses retranslated mundane illustrations into pure form. Her figures bear no stylistic resemblance to the images from which they are derived. Because they are conceived abstractly rather than three-dimensionally, at a certain level they are better perceived in compositional than human terms. They are not intrinsically lifelike, but are rather given life by their painted surroundings and their interaction with each other. Above all, it is the strength and immediacy of the Moses landscape that provides her paintings with their emotional impact. The little vignettes serve to anchor the landscape—to place it in a social context and

explain its practical function as a sphere of human activity. Visually, they act as a foil to the more complex tones of their natural environment and as compositional and spatial guideposts.

The artist created a paper-doll world, peopled not by real creatures, but by symbols of real creatures. Thereby she demanded a role of the imagination similar to that found in child's play. Her viewers are invited to finish the story, cued by details of place and occupation. The sphere of action is thus removed from a personal to a universal plane. What these people do—the stroll through the meadow, the struggle with laundry before an imminent storm, the invigorating frolic in the snow—is known to us all, even though the Moses characters lack identity. The accuracy of the landscape makes their peregrinations real, and we become them.

150. **Blacksmith Shop.** 1951. 16″ x 28″. Formerly collection Forrest K. Moses. (K. 996)

151. **"Trotting Cracks"
at the Forge.** 1869.
Lithograph. Published
by Currier and Ives,
New York. The
Library of Congress,
Washington, D.C.

152. **The Meeting House.** 1949. 18¾″ x 26¼″. (K. 878).

Interiors

Grandma Moses was chiefly a landscape painter, and for this reason interiors always gave her difficulties. Still, she got a number of requests for such subjects, and to some extent felt obliged to comply with them. "I tried that interior," she wrote Kallir's assistant, Hildegard Bachert, "but did not like it, so I erased it, that don't seem to be in my line, I like to paint something that leads me on and on into the unknown, something that I want to see away on beyond. Well, maybe I try again."[144] She had an almost psychological inability to visualize an interior without simultaneously imagining its exterior. The juxtaposition of interior and exterior views seen from within an open barn was a device used in some Currier and Ives prints (Plate 151). Moses employed a similar method in her version of *Blacksmith Shop* (Plate 150), but here, as in her painting *Pumpkins* (Plate 153), she insisted on

placing the barn itself in an outdoor setting. This led to a cutaway, dollhouselike depiction of the buildings, with furnishings and activities spilling out to merge with the landscape.

Moses did, of course, paint some successful interiors, which are highly prized by many for their comparatively "primitive" qualities. At their best, these were complex arabesques of brightly colored block forms—exercises in two-dimensional design with a genuine charm of their own. Paintings like *The Meeting House* (Plate 152) or *Christmas at Home* (Plate 154) lack the depth and technical sophistication of the artist's landscapes. However, as distillations of form and basically abstract compositional arrangements, they are unmatched in her oeuvre.

153. **Pumpkins.** 1959. 16″ x 24″. (K. 1380). Confused perspective typifies Moses' interiors. Here we look into the barn through a missing front wall, out through a back door, and, simultaneously, we see the wider landscape that surrounds the entire building.

154. **Christmas at Home.** 1946. 18″ x 23″. Private collection. (K. 586).

155. **Bondsville Fair.** 1945. 18″ x 23¼″. Collection Bill Johnson. (K. 497). A counterpart to Moses' interiors were her outdoor activity scenes. Both types of painting involved complex figural groupings, but she definitely preferred the latter.

Social Events

Certain social activities demanded an indoor setting, but the artist clearly preferred depicting those that took place outside. Though both types of composition emphasized the arrangement of multiple figural groupings, the exterior approach allowed for more variety of scale. The confined space of *The Quilting Bee* (Plate 156) contrasts sharply with the panoramic view of *Bondsville Fair* (Plate 155). As do all the artist's landscapes, the latter relies on variations in size to denote distance, while in the interior the characters are relatively uniform. For all its seeming bustle, the quilting scene is uncharacteristically static. The *Fair*, on the other hand, retains the airiness and rhythmic flow one associates with the Moses style.

156. **The Quilting Bee.** 1950. 20″ x 24″. Private collection. (K. 883). The artist could not resist adding an ample view of the outside scenery as a backdrop.

157. **So Long Till Next Year.** 1960. 16″ x 24″. Grandma Moses Properties, New York. (K. 1461).

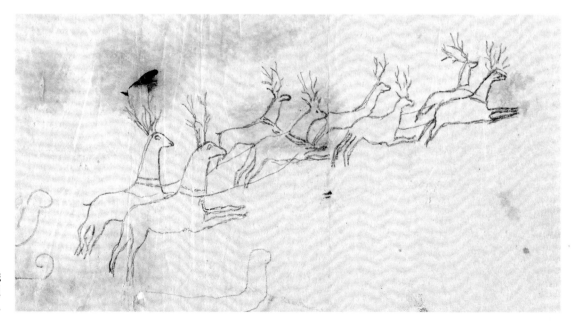

158. Study for **So Long Till Next Year.** Pencil on thin paper. 7⅜″ x 9¼″.

CHAPTER FIVE

ARTISTIC GROWTH

Versatility

Grandma Moses painted every day. Berry-picking, sock-darning, and cookie-baking—the sort of activities that had once ruled her life—now took second place to her art. She would not have been able to express in words what it meant to her to be a painter. Otto Kallir put it succinctly in a radio interview two days after her death: "Painting kept her alive. The moment she couldn't paint any more, she died."[145]

By the time of her first show in 1940, the artist had probably created about 100 small paintings, and half again as many worsted pictures. Because comparatively little of her time was devoted to making preliminary drawings, she was able to channel her full energy into the paintings themselves. It is therefore not surprising that over the decades she produced an oeuvre of some 1600 works. One of the benefits of her arrangement with Kallir's Galerie St. Etienne was that it freed her from the pressures of working to order, allowing her to paint at her own pace and according to her own inclinations. Thus she was not hindered from varying both the quantity and the content of her output, and was able to move away from especially popular subjects when she felt she had exhausted them.

Moses remained ever open to new suggestions. The novelty of painting on ceramic tiles, for example, appealed to her, and encouraged by a friend, she happily took up the technique at the age of ninety-one. The challenge of an unfamiliar situation sparked her creative ingenuity. Unable to devise elaborate tonal arrangements with the thick ceramic paint, she concentrated on the application of line and solid form (Plate 159). Similarly, her venture into children's book illustration inspired unexpected innovation. Toward the end

159. **Grandma is Coming.** Circa 1951–52. Ceramic tile. 6″ x 6″. (K. Tile 12).

of her life, Moses finally gave in to Kallir's prodding and agreed to illustrate *The Night Before Christmas*. The subject—children and houses in winter—was not so unusual for her, but the fantasy element of the story demanded special treatment. The artist studied reindeer (Plate 158) as carefully as she had once studied common farm animals, but her total approach transcended anything she had attempted previously. Trees were etched in crystalline wisps of white on bright-hued backgrounds to create a magical wonderland setting for the children's holiday dreams (Plate 157).

160. **Sugaring Off in Maple Orchard.** 1940. Oil on canvas. 18⅛″ x 24⅛″. Private collection. (K. 56). Moses combined memories of youthful sugaring parties with an established pictorial tradition for one of her most popular and sustained series of "theme" paintings. The nucleus grouping of the log cabin and steaming cauldron originated with Currier and Ives (Plate 162).

161. **Sugaring Off in Maple Orchard** (detail). The artist seems to have had difficulty reconciling her flat shapes with a desire to articulate details such as clothing.

Early Work

Because Moses worked for several decades, her style displayed the depth of development one is accustomed to find in the work of practicing artists. This can be illustrated graphically by a comparison of her treatment of the "sugaring off" scene at different points in her career. "Sugaring" was one of the few standard themes that remained interesting to her over the years, probably because it permitted an endless variety of figural and landscape combinations. The subject itself was an old one. Or, at least, it was as old as Currier and Ives (Plate 162). While Moses does not seem to have executed a verbatim copy of the original print, it did serve as a nucleus for several of her initial renditions of the

subject (Plate 160). Yet even at this time she was expanding the landscape element in a unique way and interpolating a cast of characters that would be featured in future "sugarings": men with buckets, the cauldron of maple syrup, the wagon of logs. In early versions, a curtain of bare trees obscures the horizon, although the artist is already trying to carve a path through them to reach the distant views she craves (Plate 163). She is also beginning to build up textures and atmospheric effects. Her figures evidence some cursory attempts at modeling; she seems torn between a desire for more realism and an urge to simplify.

162. **Maple Sugaring—Early Spring in the Northern Woods.** 1872. Lithograph. Published by Currier and Ives, New York. The Harry T. Peters Collection; Museum of the City of New York. Parts of this print can be identified in many of the artist's "sugarings," though she never copied it exactly.

163. Sugaring Off in Maple Orchard (detail, Plate 160). The unusually heavy texture of this work heightens the tonal interplay.

164. Sugaring Off in Maple Orchard (detail, Plate 160). Here, inadequate control of the viscous paint resulted in a coarsening of detail.

165. **Sugaring Off.** 1943. 23″ x 27″. Estate of Otto Kallir. (K. 276). Integration of multiple elements in an almost unnaturally vast landscape was the hallmark of the "Grandma Moses style."

166. **Sugaring Off** (detail). The same configuration seen in Plate 164 is here delicately defined.

167. **Sugaring Off** (detail).

Mature Style

Within just a few years, Moses had evolved her distinctive landscape style. The background hills are thrown wide open in a *Sugaring Off* of 1943 (Plate 165). The scene is deeper and far more involved than in earlier renditions, without sacrificing compositional unity. The artist has learned to weave the various figural elements into a cohesive pattern and to intertwine them with the landscape so that the latter becomes an integral pictorial component rather than a backdrop. As one moves up the picture plane, anecdotal elements decrease in number, the receding distance clearly denoted by their diminishing size. More distant figures have become distinctly stylized, with little effort at detail (Plate 167). For close-ups, the artist has achieved a unity of block form articulated by crisp details, giving her both the illusion of reality and the purity of design she had been seeking (Plate 166). Her application of paint is flatter than previously, and she is able, perhaps partly on account of better brushes, to obtain a precision that once eluded her. She is inclined to see shapes in formal rather than representational terms, so that, for example, the thrust of a boy's arm is incorporated as a dynamic configuration, not an anatomical movement (Plate 168).

168. **Sugaring Off** (detail).

Continuing Development

Once she had achieved a satisfactory solution to the initial dilemma of combining natural and human elements, the artist began to experiment with variations of approach. Again, it is instructive to examine her "sugarings," for they mirror developments that are applicable to her work as a whole. In a *Sugaring Off* of 1955 (Plate 169), for example, she allowed the anecdotal elements to take over, so that even the trees function primarily as components in a frenetic dance of color and shape. The hues are unusually bright, with gay green buckets as repeated color accents. In works like this, the artist was pushing the possibilities inherent in her anecdotal structuring to their logical extreme, an extreme that she would eventually reject. Of more relevance to her later development is the pronounced loosening of brushwork. Forms are becoming increasingly simplified; the original Currier and Ives vignette is rendered in miniature on the upper left side (Plate 170). Figures, especially in the distance, are hardly more than fleeting dabs of paint (Plate 171). There is a sudden note of crudeness reminiscent of the artist's early work. However, whereas formerly this was the result of inadequate technical resources, now it was created deliberately, with instinctive sureness of effect. Having mastered the basic geometric configurations that made up her subjects, Moses was able to abbreviate them confidently.

The extremely broad landscape was the hallmark of the Grandma Moses style, but it had its limitations. Because of its dependence on overall patterning, this sort of composition tended to stress all its pictorial ingredients equally. Certain subjects required a more pointed focus (see, for example, *Joy Ride*, Plate 88, or *The Thunderstorm*, Plate 132), so the artist began to adapt her methods to a contracted framework. The horizontal format of *Maple Bush* (Plate 172), painted in 1953, encourages a roughly even division across the center between landscape and figures. The emphasis on pattern has been reduced and replaced by a concern with paint texture. Elements have become more compact, space more concentrated. The stylistic compression of this painting, observable in both the composition and the rendering of its individual constituents, anticipates some of the qualities that would distinguish Moses' late work.

169. **Sugaring Off.** 1955. 18″ x 24″. (K. 1166). The artist seems to have been trying to assemble as many vignettes as possible, yet the "Moses framework" holds the images together.

170. **Sugaring Off** (detail, Plate 169). The basic ingredients of the Currier and Ives composition (Plate 162) have been reduced to minute dabs of pigment.

171. **Sugaring Off** (detail, Plate 169).

172. **Maple Bush.** 1953. 12″ x 18″. Formerly collection Louis J. Caldor. (K. 1088).

173. **Sugar Time.** 1960. 16″ x 24″. (K. 1468).

174. **Sugar Time** (detail). Increased compression of the background landscape encourages increased stylistic compression of formal configurations.

Painterly Abandon

The trends implied by *Sugaring Off* and *Maple Bush* came to bold fruition in Moses' later work. The balance between the linear and the painterly tipped toward the painterly. She abandoned formal patterning in favor of textural structure. Her predilection for narrower horizontals became pronounced. Space was no longer defined by an elaborate interweaving of landscape and figures carefully coordinated by diminishing size. There were fewer figures and fewer spatial gradations. The action centered in the foreground, which now occupied most of the lower half of the panel, forcing the condensation of the receding background distance into a much tighter band than in previous work.

Gradually, the paint took over Moses' compositions. Figures are rendered with a few loose strokes in *Sugar Time* (Plate 174). The trees are subsumed by a haze of color and pigment that threatens to engulf the more distant houses (Plate 173). A preliminary sketch (Plate 176) for a slightly earlier painting of the same title (Plate 175) reveals a new extreme of stylization. Reformulating this penciled image in paint, the artist adhered only loosely to its original boundaries, freely violating them with her fluid brushwork. The unfinished *Sugaring Off* of 1960 (Plate 177) exposes her working method most advantageously: one sees clearly a growing conflict between line and texture. A thick coat of snow virtually obscures the sparse branches of the trees. While the background, in particular, is the site of a nearly expressionistic frenzy, the cows in the foreground remain docile within their simple pencil contours (Plate 178).

No matter how old an artist is when he or she dies, there is always a temptation to wonder, "What would have happened next?" It is quite clear that toward the end of Moses' life, texture was conquering line in her work. In her very last "sugarings," all the figures are rendered solely in terms of paint and color, with no attempt to follow a neatly conceived outline (Plate 180). Her shorthand technique, with its increased emphasis on the intrinsic qualities of pigment, hue, and form, makes explicit the abstract tendencies implicit in her work from the start.

175. **Sugar Time.** 1960. 16″ x 24″. (K.1440). A modified version of the Currier and Ives print (Plate 162) has been used in the foreground.

176. Study for **Sugar Time** (Plate 175). Pencil on thin paper. 2⅜″ x 10¼″. Note the reappearance of the horse and sleigh from Plates 164 and 166.

177. **Sugaring Off.** 1960. 16″ x 24″. (Unfinished). (K. 1448).

178. **Sugaring Off** (detail).

179. **Vermont Sugar.** 1961. 16″ x 24″. (K. 1496). In the artist's last works, line is almost entirely obliterated by pigment.

180. **Vermont Sugar** (detail). Moses developed a shorthand technique in which loose brushwork was used to suggest rather than to define images.

181. **Eagle Bridge Hotel.** 1959. 16″ x 24″. (K. 1387). This picture was executed about six months before the artist's 100th birthday.

The Late Style

In part, one may be tempted to seek an explanation for the changes in Moses' late work in her attempt to control a growing unsteadiness of hand. It is apparent, however, that the artist was quite aware of what she was doing and that it was intentional. "I'm changing my style," she said in a 1956 interview, "getting modern in my old age, with a head full of ideas."[146] The late style was not a diminishment but a triumph of her creativity. It had the effect of reducing the anecdotal aspect of her subjects and concentrating the expressive impact. Pattern became less important than painterly unity. Hue and texture became dominant, with increased emphasis on atmospheric effects. The figural elements were rendered with fluid brushwork rather than as flat shapes. They began to merge with the background, so that both became integral components in a network of pigment and color.

Grandma Moses had journeyed, in her twenty-odd years as a painter, from the objective perception of nature to the subjective experience of it. Old age may have contributed to the change by turning her more inside herself, prompting her to rely more on memory than direct observation, to regard her art more exclusively in terms of her immediate materials: the color, the paint, and the painter herself. It is significant that Emily Genauer called Moses' last finished painting, *Rainbow* (Plate 184), "a statement about the inner artist."[147] Color is used here, as in Moses' other late work, in a way more purely expressive than representationally accurate. The exuberant swish of the scythes, candy-striped in yellow, white, and red, and the spun-sugar puff of pink flowers, out of which a hay wagon rises like a small triumphant chariot (Plate 186), are presented as bright symbols in paint, tokens of peace, an offering of hope. A painting like this is a direct outpouring of the artist's spirit as well as a technical *tour de force* of color and texture.

182. **Horses and Carriage.** Pencil on thin paper. 3¼″ x 5¼″. Moses' late drawings reflect a softening of form similar to that observed in her paintings.

183. **Eagle Bridge Hotel** (detail).

184. **Rainbow.** 1961. 16″ x
24″. (K 1511).

185. **Rainbow** (detail).

Conclusion

Style is a product neither of instantaneous inspiration nor of plodding imitation. Folk painters do not concoct style out of thin air any more than academic artists achieve greatness merely by adopting the precepts of their predecessors. Self-taught artists do not have more lenient teachers than the school-taught. They have the same strict master all artists have: themselves. And, like the academic artist, they must also seek guidance from work done by others. They too have a visual heritage, albeit a makeshift one, that supports them. They are compilers of information and experience; they are inventors and creators. They evolve style in exactly the same way that all artists do, but they evolve it without the benefit of an academic education. They exist, therefore, outside tradition; they must create their own.

In America in the 1940s, an elderly widow set about the serious task of teaching herself to paint. She had nothing to guide her other than the well-meaning but often meaningless advice of strangers and a sure sense of what was pleasing to her eye. Some praised what she had painted, and some criticized it. To the old lady in Eagle Bridge, it made little difference. A hundred years after her birth, she had survived a civil war and two world wars to become, herself, a part of history. She was, as the saying goes, a legend in her own lifetime. From the point of view of a public war-battered to the point of despair, Grandma Moses could not have come at a better time. For the champions of the American avant-garde, her timing could not have been worse. Amidst a flurry of theories and high-flown aesthetic debates, the artist created paintings that were simple, direct recollections of a life almost everyone could relate to. The concerns of sophisticated art circles were not her concerns. What she was up to had nothing to do with theories or fashion, and everything to do with art.

186. **Rainbow** (detail).

BIOGRAPHICAL CHRONOLOGY

Including a selection of major exhibitions and publications.

1860 September 7: Anna Mary Robertson is born in Greenwich, New York, the third of ten children of Mary Shannahan and Russell King Robertson, a farmer.

1872 Leaves home to work as "hired girl" on neighboring farm. Will spend most of next fifteen years in this manner, learning to sew, cook, and keep house.

1870s Obtains a few years of schooling along with the children of family for which she works.

1887 November 9: Marries Thomas Salmon Moses.

1887– The couple lives and farms in Virginia. Mrs. Moses contrib-
1905 utes to family income by producing butter and potato chips. Ten children are born; five die in infancy.

1905 The family returns to New York State, purchasing a farm in Eagle Bridge.

1909 February: Her mother dies.
June: Her father dies.

1918 Paints first large picture on the fireboard in the parlor.

Ca. Paints landscapes on the panels of her "tip-up" table and
1920 occasional pictures for relatives and friends.

1927 January 15: Thomas Salmon Moses dies.

1932 Goes to Bennington, Vermont, to assist ailing daughter Anna. After Anna's death, she stays on to care for two grandchildren.

1935 Returns to Eagle Bridge. Begins to paint in earnest. Exhibits pictures at local events, such as fairs and charity sales.

1938 Display of her pictures in Thomas's Drugstore, Hoosick Falls, N.Y., discovered by Louis J. Caldor.

1939 October 18–November 18: Three paintings included in show of "Contemporary Unknown American Painters" in the Members' Rooms, Museum of Modern Art, New York (Checklist: Introduction by Sidney Janis).

1940 October 9–31: First one-woman show, "What a Farm Wife Painted," Galerie St. Etienne, New York.
November: Visits New York to attend exhibition of her work at Gimbels Thanksgiving Festival.

187. Grandma Moses and Carolyn Thomas at Gimbels Auditorium. November 14, 1940.

1941 Receives New York State Prize for *Old Oaken Bucket* at the Syracuse Museum of Fine Arts (now Everson Museum of Art), Syracuse, New York. The painting is purchased by Thomas J. Watson, founder of IBM.

1942 Chapter devoted to Grandma Moses in *They Taught Themselves* by Sidney Janis (New York: The Dial Press).
February 9–March 7: Three paintings included in exhibition of the same title, Marie Harriman Gallery, New York (Catalogue: Statement by André Breton).
December 7–22: "Anna Mary Robertson Moses: Loan Exhibition of Paintings," American British Art Center, New York.

1944 February: "New Paintings by Grandma Moses–The Senior of the American Primitives," Galerie St. Etienne, New York.
December: "Grandma Moses," Galerie St. Etienne, New York.

1944– Traveling exhibitions, usually comprising about twenty
1963 Moses pictures, organized annually and shown in cities throughout the United States (Alabama, California, Connecticut, Delaware, District of Columbia, Florida, Illinois, Indiana, Iowa, Kansas, Louisiana, Maryland, Massachusetts, Minnesota, Missouri, Montana, Nebraska, New Hampshire, New York, North Carolina, Ohio, Oklahoma, Pennsylvania, South Carolina, Tennessee, Texas, Vermont, Virginia, Washington, Wisconsin).

1945 November 13–18: "Women's International Exposition: Woman's Life in Peacetime," Madison Square Garden, New York. One-woman show; attended by Grandma Moses.

1945– Represented in annual juried exhibition of the Carnegie
1950 Institute, Pittsburgh, Pa.

1946 Publication of *Grandma Moses, American Primitive*, edited by Otto Kallir, with introduction by Louis Bromfield and autobiographical notes by Grandma Moses (New York: The Dryden Press).
First Moses Christmas cards published.

1947 Second edition of *Grandma Moses, American Primitive*, with more color plates (Garden City, N.Y.: Doubleday & Co.).
May 17–June 14: One-woman exhibition, Galerie St. Etienne, New York (Catalogue: *How Do I Paint?* by Grandma Moses).
The Hallmark Company begins long-term policy of publishing Moses Christmas and greeting cards.

1948 First large color reproductions produced by the Arthur Jaffe Heliochrome Co., New York.
Thanksgiving–Christmas: "Ten Years Grandma Moses," Galerie St. Etienne, New York (Catalogue: *I Remember* by Grandma Moses).

1949 February: Her youngest son, Hugh, dies.
May: The Women's National Press Club Award "For Outstanding Accomplishment In Art" presented to her by President Harry S Truman in Washington, D.C.
May 8–June 9: "Paintings by Grandma Moses," The Phillips Gallery, Washington, D.C.
June: Receives Honorary Doctorate from Russell Sage College, Troy, N.Y.

188. Grandma Moses and Otto Kallir in Eagle Bridge. 1944.

Included in *Pictorial Folk Art in America, New England to California* by Alice Ford (New York and London: The Studio Publications, Inc.).

1950 Documentary color film produced by Jerome Hill with narration by Archibald MacLeish, photography by Erica Anderson.
June–December: First Moses exhibitions shown in Europe under the auspices of the U.S. Information Service (Vienna, Munich, Salzburg, Berne, The Hague, Paris).
September 7–October 15: "Grandma Moses: Exhibition Arranged on the Occasion of Her 90th Birthday," Albany Institute of History and Art, Albany, N.Y.
Included in *Primitive Painters in America* by Jean Lipman and Alice Winchester (New York: Dodd, Mead & Co.).

1951 April: Moves from her old farm to more comfortable one-story house across the road. Her daughter, Winona Fisher, takes over running of household.
March: Receives Honorary Doctorate from the Moore Institute of Art, Philadelphia, Pa.

1952 Publication of *My Life's History* by Grandma Moses, edited by Otto Kallir (New York: Harper & Row/London: André Deutsch/Frankfurt am Main: Ullstein Verlag, 1957/Utrecht: A.W. Bruna & Zoon, 1958).
December: Publication of *Christmas* by Grandma Moses (New York: Galerie St. Etienne).

1953 October 20: Moses is guest speaker at *The New York Herald Tribune* Forum in New York.

1954– Five paintings included in "American Primitive Paintings
1955 from the 17th Century to the Present," exhibition organized for circulation in Europe by the Smithsonian Institution for the U.S. Information Agency (Lucerne, Vienna, Munich, Dortmund, Stockholm, Oslo, Manchester, London, Trier).

1955 June: Edward R. Murrow interviews her for his "See It Now" series, telecast December 13.
November 29–December 31: "A Tribute to Grandma Moses," on the occasion of her 95th birthday, presented by Thomas J. Watson and the Fine Arts Department of the International Business Machines Corp., IBM Gallery, New York (Catalogue: Tribute by Thomas J. Watson; *Work and Happiness* and *My Tip-Up Table* by Grandma Moses). Moses travels to New York to attend opening.

1956 Painting specially commissioned by President Eisenhower's cabinet is given to him on the third anniversary of his inauguration.
Publication of set of four color reproductions, "The Four Seasons" (Port Chester, N.Y.: Donald Art Company).

1957 May 6–June 4: "Grandma Moses: New York Showing of an Exhibition Presented in Europe During 1955–1957," Galerie St. Etienne, New York (Catalogue: *Grandma Moses* by Hubertus, Prince zu Löwenstein; excerpts from European reviews).

1958 October 14: Her daughter, Winona Fisher, dies. Son Forrest and his wife move into the house to take care of her.

1959 Included in *Modern Primitives: Masters of Naïve Painting* by Oto Bihalji-Merin (New York: Harry N. Abrams, Inc.). Publication of portfolio of six color reproductions, "Six of My Favorite Paintings" (New York: Catalda Fine Arts, Inc.).

1960 September 7: Governor Nelson A. Rockefeller proclaims the artist's birthday "Grandma Moses Day" in New York State.
September 12–October 6: "My Life's History: A Loan Exhibition of Paintings by Grandma Moses," on the occasion of her 100th birthday, organized at the IBM Gallery, New York (Catalogue: Tributes by Governor Nelson A. Rockefeller, Otto Kallir, Jean Cassou; autobiographical notes by Grandma Moses).

1960– "My Life's History" exhibition circulated by the Smithsonian
1961 Institution (Milwaukee, Washington, D.C., Chattanooga, Baton Rouge, Seattle, Laguna Beach, Fort Worth, Winnipeg, Chicago).

1961 July 18: Grandma Moses is taken to Health Center in Hoosick Falls, N.Y.
September 7: Governor Nelson A. Rockefeller again proclaims "Grandma Moses Day" in New York State.
Publication of *The Grandma Moses Storybook*, containing stories and poems by 28 writers, edited by Nora Kramer and illustrated by Grandma Moses, with biographical sketch by Otto Kallir (New York: Random House).
December 13: Grandma Moses dies at the Health Center.

POSTHUMOUS PUBLICATIONS, HONORS, AND EXHIBITIONS

1962 Publication of Clement C. Moore's *The Night Before Christmas*, with illustrations painted by Grandma Moses in 1960 (New York: Random House).
November–December: "Grandma Moses: Memorial Exhibition," Galerie St. Etienne, New York (Catalogue: *On the Style and Technique of Grandma Moses* by Otto Kallir).

1962– "A Life's History in 40 Pictures," traveling exhibition circu-
1964 lated in Europe (Vienna, Paris, Bremen, Hamburg, Hameln, Fulda, Düsseldorf, Darmstadt, Mannheim, Berlin, Frankfurt, Oslo, Stockholm, Helsinki, Gothenburg, Copenhagen, Moscow) and concluded at Hammer Galleries, New York.

1964 July–October: Two paintings included in exhibition "De Lusthof der Naïeven"/"Le Monde des Naifs," Museum Boymans-van Beuningen, Rotterdam; Musée National d'Art Moderne, Paris (Catalogue: Essays by Jean Cassou, J.C. Ebbinge Wubben, and Oto Bihalji-Merin).

1966 July 26–October 2: Eleven paintings included in the "1st Triennial of Insitic Art," Slovenska Národná Galéria, Bratislava (Catalogue).

1966– Forrest and Mary Moses acquire one-room schoolhouse
1972 where Anna Mary attended classes and have it moved to the old Moses farm in Eagle Bridge; they remodel interior and exhibit mementos of Grandma Moses' life.

1967 Publication of portfolio of eight color reproductions, with appreciation by John Canaday (New York: Art in America).

1968– "The Grandma Moses Gallery," continuous display of paint-
1972 ings and documentary material at the Bennington Museum, Bennington, Vermont.

1969 February 20–March 30: "Art and Life of Grandma Moses," loan exhibition of 151 pictures, the "tip-up" table, and documentary material, The Gallery of Modern Art, New York. Catalogue by Otto Kallir (New York: Gallery of Modern Art/South Brunswick and New York: A.S. Barnes/London: Thomas Yoseloff, Ltd).
May 1: Six-cent Grandma Moses commemorative stamp issued by the United States Government. Stamp depicts detail of the painting *July Fourth*, owned by the White House. Publication of *Grandma Moses, Favorite Painter* by Charles Graves (Champaign, Ill.: Garrard Publishing Co.).

1971 Publication of *Barefoot in the Grass: The Story of Grandma Moses* by William H. Armstrong (Garden City, N.Y.: Doubleday & Co.).

1972 February 22–March 11: Fifteen paintings included in "Four American Primitives: Edward Hicks, John Kane, Anna Mary Robertson Moses, Horace Pippin," ACA Galleries, New York (Catalogue: Essays by Andrew J. Crispo, Leon Anthony Arkus, Otto Kallir, and Selden Rodman).

189. The Moses clan gather in front of the Eagle Bridge farmhouse to celebrate the artist's 87th birthday. September 7, 1947. Photograph courtesy Mrs. Hugh W. Moses.

1973 Publication of *Grandma Moses* by Otto Kallir, including a catalogue raisonné (New York: Harry N. Abrams, Inc.) Publication of four color reproductions (New York: American Heritage Publishing Company).

1973– Bennington Museum annexes Grandma Moses schoolhouse as
pres. supplement to continuing display of paintings and related memorabilia.

1974– November–March: Five paintings included in "Die Kunst
1975 der Naïven," Haus der Kunst, Munich; Kunsthaus, Zurich (Catalogue: Oto Bihalji-Merin).

1975 Publication of concise edition of Otto Kallir's *Grandma Moses* (New York: Harry N. Abrams, Inc. and New American

Library/Cologne: M. DuMont Schauberg; pocketbook edition, DuMont Buchverlag, 1979/Amsterdam: Meulenhoff).

1979 February 11–April 1: "Grandma Moses, Anna Mary Robertson Moses (1860–1961)," loan exhibition of 43 paintings, National Gallery of Art, Washington, D.C. (Catalogue: Introduction by J. Carter Brown; tributes by Jean Cassou and Archibald MacLeish; quotes from Grandma Moses' writings).

1981– November 17–January 9: Seven paintings included in "The
1982 Folk Art Tradition: Naïve Painting in Europe and the United States," Galerie St. Etienne, New York. Catalogue by Jane Kallir; Foreword by Dr. Robert Bishop (New York: Galerie St. Etienne and The Viking Press/London: Allen Lane Ltd).

NOTES

1. Allen H. Eaton, "Meadows and Wildwood of Grandma Moses, Her Life and Work Into Her 102nd Year" (unpublished manuscript).

2. Grandma Moses, *My Life's History,* ed. Otto Kallir (New York: Harper & Row, Publishers, 1952), p. 34 (hereafter cited as *History*).

3. Ibid., pp. 41-42.

4. Ibid., p. 26.

5. Ibid., p. 27.

6. Eaton, op. cit., Part V, p. 1.

7. Ibid., Part I, p. 6.

8. Moses, *History*, p. 91.

9. Among the items carefully preserved by Martha Eaton in connection with her late father's manuscript is a promissory note from Thomas, dated July 17, 1898, confirming a loan of $360.00, with interest, from his wife.

10. Eaton, op. cit., Part VI, p. 36.

11. Ibid., Part VI, p. 35.

12. Moses, *History*, p. 129.

13. Eaton, op. cit., Part I, pp. 6–7.

14. Louis J. Caldor, letter to Otto Kallir, July 3, 1951.

15. Ibid.

16. Louis J. Caldor, letter to Anna Mary Robertson Moses, March 20, 1939.

17. Louis J. Caldor, letter to Anna Mary Robertson Moses, October 3, 1939.

18. Louis J. Caldor, letter to Anna Mary Robertson Moses, October 19, 1939.

19. Sidney Janis, *They Taught Themselves* (New York: The Dial Press, 1942).

20. Barbara Rose, *American Art Since 1900, A Critical History* (New York: Frederick A. Praeger, Publishers, 1967), p. 11.

21. Howard Devree, untitled article, *The New York Times,* October 13, 1940.

22. "Grandma Moses Just Paints and Makes No Fuss About It," *The New York World-Telegram,* November 15, 1940.

23. Anna Mary Robertson Moses, letter to Louis J. Caldor, February 1942. One should note here that the many towns mentioned by Moses were chiefly small places in upstate New York; her renown had not yet spread to other parts of the country.

24. Anna Mary Robertson Moses, letter to Louis J. Caldor, February 28, 1941.

25. Anna Mary Robertson Moses, letter to Louis J. Caldor, October 11, 1940.

26. Anna Mary Robertson Moses, letter to Louis J. Caldor, February 1942.

27. Anna Mary Robertson Moses, letter to Louis J. Caldor, April 28, 1941.

28. N.H., letter to Anna Mary Robertson Moses, February 24, 1944.

29. Anna Mary Robertson Moses, letter to Otto Kallir, February 21, 1944.

30. Sidney Janis, letter to Anna Mary Robertson Moses, December 4, 1944.

31. Toward the end of 1941, the artist's brother, Fred E. Robertson, himself a would-be painter of some talent, had given her a book in which to record her paintings. He also gave her a supply of printed labels, which were to be dated, numbered, and titled in accordance with the entries in the record book, and applied to the back of each painting. Moses adhered to this procedure erratically at first but eventually learned to systematically keep track of her output.

32. Anna Mary Robertson Moses, letter to Otto Kallir, November 14, 1944.

33. Anna Mary Robertson Moses, letter to Edward Moses, April 16, 1950.

34. Moses, *History*, p. 138.

35. Anna Wetherill Olmsted, "She Found Her Metier at the Age of 79," *Syracuse* [New York] *Post-Standard,* September 17, 1944.

36. Bob Hope, "It's the Spirit," *Chicago Times,* January 17, 1946.

37. Bernice Breen, "Life Begins at Eighty," *Milady, The South African Journal for Smart Women,* December 1946.

38. Laura Scott Meyers, untitled article, *El Paso* [Texas] *Herald-Post,* June 27, 1947.

39. Josephine Lowman, "Why Grow Old? Grandma Moses' Talent for Living," *Oakland* [California] *Tribune,* July 3, 1949.

40. Ernestine Evans, "Untaught, She Painted What She Loved," *The New York Herald Tribune Weekly Book Review,* December 22, 1946.

41. John Erskine, "Author John Erskine Reviews Grandma Moses' Autobiography," *The New York Journal-American,* January 12, 1947.

42. Molly Matson, "Molly Tells—Paints First Picture at 84, New York Farm Woman Gains National Fame in Art," *The Conshohoken* [Pennsylvania] *Recorder,* September 6, 1946.

43. H.A., letter to Anna Mary Robertson Moses, February 4, 1945.

44. J.R., letter to Anna Mary Robertson Moses, April 23, 1947.

45. H.S., comment in the guestbook for the exhibition "A Tribute to Grandma Moses," IBM Gallery of Arts and Sciences, New York, 1955.

46. Elizabeth Shelton, "Grandma Moses, 88, Here to Get Art Award, Finds Contrast with Her Honeymoon Capital," *Washington D.C. Times Herald,* May 15, 1949.

47. Ibid.

48. Frank Sullivan, "An Afternoon with Grandma Moses," *The New York Times Magazine,* October 9, 1949.

49. Jess Stearn, "If Grandma Moses Can Do It . . . Everybody Is Painting Now, and We Don't Mean Houses," *New York News,* November 27, 1949.

50. Grace Davidson, "Many Now Paint as Escape—Artist Zerbe Sees Effort to Forget Atomic Age," *Boston Post,* October 28, 1949.

51. "Grandma Moses Sees Her Paintings Telecast," *Hoosick Falls* [New York] *Standard Press,* December 1948.

52. Otto Kallir, *Grandma Moses* (New York: Harry N. Abrams, Inc., 1973), pp. 173–175 (hereafter cited as *Moses*).

53. Irving Sandler, *The Triumph of American Painting: A History of Abstract Expressionism* (New York: Praeger Publishers, 1970).

54. Aline Saarinen, "American Art Abroad—Paris Finds Paintings Controversial, But the Big Show Proves Popular," *The New York Times,* April 17, 1955.

55. Aline B. Louchheim, "Americans in Italy—Biennale Representation Raises Many Issues," *The New York Times,* September 10, 1950.

56. *Hamburger Echo,* Hamburg, Germany, February 21, 1956, reprinted in *Grandma Moses: New York Showing of an Exhibition of Paintings Presented in Europe During 1955–57* (New York: Galerie St. Etienne, 1957), p. 15 (hereafter cited as *GSE 1957*).

57. *Ludwigsburger Kreiszeitung,* Ludwigsburg, Germany, December 13, 1955, reprinted in *GSE 1957,* p. 13.

58. Ibid., p. 12.

59. *Art News and Review,* England, April 28, 1956, reprinted in *GSE 1957,* pp. 17–18.

60. Sandler, op. cit., p. 1.

61. "The Realists' Predicament—Past and Present Traditions of the National Scene," *The* [London] *Times Literary Supplement,* November 6, 1959.

62. Saul Pett, "Grandma Moses, 90 This Week and Feeling Fine, Sniffs at Art Fame and Keeps Right on Painting," *Tulsa* [Oklahoma] *World,* September 3, 1950.

63. Otto Kallir, ed., *Grandma Moses, American Primitive* (New York: The Dryden Press, 1946), p. 15.

64. J.M., letter to the editor, *Time,* January 18, 1954.

65. "Grandma Moses—Good for Her!" *Manchester* [New Hampshire] *Union,* October 11, 1949.

66. "About Grandma Moses," *The New York World-Telegram,* May 21, 1947.

67. "The Low Down," *Oakland* [California] *Neighborhood Journal,* November 23, 1949.

68. Sandler, op. cit., pp. 29–30.

69. Moses, *History,* p. 45.

70. Ibid., p. 30.

71. Nanette Kutner, "Grandma Moses' Secret," *The American Weekly,* September 6, 1953.

72. The exhibition, titled "American Painting Today—1950," was the first survey of its kind since World War II. Although five all-artist regional juries were chosen to assure fairness, a number of New York abstract artists, feeling that the dominant jurors were prejudiced against advanced art, boycotted the competition. Their protest had the effect of galvanizing the art world, prompting artists to take sides for or against the Metropolitan Museum's approach. This, in the long run, may have been more significant than the exhibition itself, which proved to be blandly comprehensive, including a number of unknowns who remained unknown.

73. "Now We Have a Ghost-Painter," *Worcester* [Massachusetts] *Gazette,* June 6, 1950.

74. "Grandma Moses No Cultist," *Lawrence* [Massachusetts] *Tribune,* December 31, 1951.

75. Ibid.

76. John Garth, "Art World," *San Francisco Argonaut,* December 11, 1952.

77. Loring Holmes Dodd, "Grandma Moses' Art Shows Rural Charm," *Worcester Gazette,* October 14, 1949.

78. Moses, *History,* p. 147.

79. "Quietness to Mark 100th Birthday of Grandma Moses," *Hoosick Falls Standard Press,* August 25, 1960.

80. Eaton, op. cit., Part I, p. 394.

81. "Grandma's Wealth to Family; World Inherits Her Paintings," *Albany* [New York] *Knickerbocker News,* January 16, 1962.

82. Harold C. Schonberg, "Grandma Moses: Portrait of the Artist at 99," *The New York Times Magazine,* September 6, 1959.

83. André Malraux, *The Voices of Silence* (Garden City, N.Y.: Doubleday & Co., Inc., 1953), p. 515.

84. Emily Genauer, "This Week in Art—Grandma Moses' Canvases Among Other Displays," *The New York World-Telegram,* March 2, 1946.

85. Emily Genauer, "This Week in Art—Granny Gains Stature as Painting Marvel," *The New York World-Telegram,* June 1, 1948.

86. Emily Genauer, "Grandma Moses: A Lovely Spirit," *The New York Herald Tribune,* September 10, 1961 (hereafter cited as "Spirit").

87. Emily Genauer, "The Passing of Grandma Moses at 101," *The New York Herald Tribune,* December 14, 1961.

88. John Canaday, "Art of Grandma Moses—An Appraisal Shows She Captured and Relayed the Magic of Being Alive," *The New York Times,* December 14, 1961.

89. Moses, *History,* p. 3.

90. Malraux, op. cit., p. 601.

91. Jean Lipman, letter to Otto Kallir, May 5, 1960. Lipman later changed her mind about Moses, choosing to omit her from a 1980 survey of American folk painting that she helped curate for the Whitney Museum of American Art.

92. "Folk" is used in this book to describe any art created outside the academic tradition, both in Europe and the United States,

in the twentieth century and earlier, because it is the word currently favored by American scholars. It must be noted, however, that most European specialists in the field heartily disagree with this broad application of the term, rather choosing to limit it to pre-modern crafts objects. "Naïve" and "primitive" are two other common adjectives, and will be used here interchangeably with "folk."

93. Jay E. Cantor, "The Landscape of Change—View of Rural New England 1790–1865," *Folk Art in America,* ed. Jack J. Ericson (New York: Mayflower Books, Inc., 1979), pp. 95–100.

94. Peter C. Marzio, *The Democratic Art—Pictures for a Nineteenth-Century America* (Boston: David R. Godine, Publisher, 1979), p. 2.

95. Ibid.

96. Howard Devree, "Two Primitives," *The New York Times,* February 13, 1944.

97. Holger Cahill, *American Folk Art—The Art of the Common Man in America, 1750–1900* (New York: The Museum of Modern Art, 1932), p. 27.

98. Robert Bishop, *Folk Painters of America* (New York: E.P. Dutton & Co., 1979), p. 14.

99. Carl W. Dreppard, "What is Primitive and What is Not?" in Ericson, op. cit., p. 12.

100. Wilhelm Uhde, *Five Primitive Masters* (New York: The Quadrangle Press, 1949), p. 53.

101. Jean Lipman, *Rufus Porter Rediscovered* (New York: Clarkson N. Potter, Inc., 1968; 1980), p. 94 (hereafter cited as *Porter*).

102. Kallir, *Moses,* p. 145.

103. Moses, *History,* p. 132.

104. Marie McSwigan, "Sky Hooks," *John Kane, Painter,* ed. Leon Anthony Arkus (Pittsburgh: University of Pittsburgh Press, 1971), p. 96.

105. Barbara C. Scott Fisher, "'Go Ahead and Paint—Anybody Can Paint if They Go About It' Says Successful Artist Grandma Moses," *The Christian Science Monitor Magazine Section,* January 5, 1946.

106. Lipman, *Porter,* p. 85.

107. McSwigan, op. cit., p. 79.

108. Ibid., p. 85.

109. Selden Rodman, *Horace Pippin—A Negro Painter in America* (New York: The Quadrangle Press, 1947), p. 80.

110. Sidney Janis, "Morris Hirshfield," *American Folk Painters of Three Centuries,* ed. Jean Lipman and Tom Armstrong (New York: Hudson Hills Press in association with the Whitney Museum of American Art, 1980), p. 193.

111. Louis J. Caldor, letter to Anna Mary Robertson Moses, November 9, 1939.

112. McSwigan, op. cit., p. 95.

113. Moses, *History,* p. 27.

114. Martha Young Hutson, *George Henry Durrie (1820–1863)* (Santa Barbara, Calif.: Santa Barbara Museum of Art and American Art Review Press, 1977), pp. 14–18.

115. Moses, *History,* p. 133.

116. Ibid.

117. The creative efforts of nineteenth-century girls and women are often preserved anonymously in household items such as samplers and quilts. Those who made more "artistic" attempts generally confined themselves to the "ladylike" media of watercolor and pastel. For the most part, even when women sold their work, it was at best a supplement to, rather than a mainstay of the family income. While it is known that Mary Ann Willson sold her watercolors to neighboring farmers, most female artists, like Eunice Pinney, probably painted chiefly for personal amusement. Occasionally, one does find record of women such as Ruth Henshaw Bascom or Ruth W. Shute, who spent parts of their lives as professional limners.

118. Moses, *History,* p. 133.

119. M.C., letter to Anna Mary Robertson Moses, September 3, 1943.

120. Sidney Janis, letter to Anna Mary Robertson Moses, May 20, 1941.

121. Anna Mary Robertson Moses, letter to Otto Kallir, November 29, 1943.

122. Anna Mary Robertson Moses, letter to Otto Kallir, March 4, 1944.

123. Anna Mary Robertson Moses, letter to Otto Kallir, November 18, 1947.

124. Moses, *History,* p. 134.

125. Anna Mary Robertson Moses, letter to Otto Kallir, November 29, 1943.

126. Ala Story, letter to Anna Mary Robertson Moses, July 30, 1943.

127. Anna Mary Robertson Moses, letter to Otto Kallir, February 21, 1944.

128. Gregory Clark, "'I Just Follow Nature' Says Grandma Moses," *Weekend Picture Magazine,* February 16, 1952.

129. Anna Mary Robertson Moses, letter to Otto Kallir, April 14, 1947.

130. Fisher, op. cit.

131. Anna Mary Robertson Moses, letter to Otto Kallir, February 21, 1944.

132. Fisher, op. cit.

133. Anna Mary Robertson Moses, letter to Otto Kallir, January 9, 1950.

134. "Grandma Moses, Painting at 87, Is 'Working Up Some Mischief,'" *The New York Herald Tribune,* August 23, 1948.

135. Margaret Breuning, "Grandma Moses," *Art Digest,* December 1, 1944.

136. Schonberg, op. cit.

137. Lipman, *Porter,* p. 97.

138. Ibid., p. 94.

139. Pett, op. cit.

140. Ibid.

141. Moses, *History,* p. 134.

142. Ibid.

143. Schonberg, op. cit.

144. Anna Mary Robertson Moses, letter to Hildegard Bachert, March 9, 1949.

145. Martha Dean interview with Otto Kallir, December 15, 1961, WOR Radio, New York.

146. Sally MacDougall, "Grandma Moses Finally Views December TV Appearance," *The New York World-Telegram and The Sun,* May 1, 1956.

147. Genauer, "Spirit."

INDEX